PICK O
PATIENCE GAMES

D1440297

PICK OF THE PACK PATIENCE GAMES

Jacqueline Harrod

RIGHT WAY

Printed and bound in Great Britain by Cox & Wyman Ltd., Reading, Berkshire.

The *Right Way* series is published by Elliot Right Way Books, Brighton Road, Lower Kingswood, Tadworth, Surrey, KT20 6TD, U.K.

CONTENTS

For Alexandra, who began it,
and Francesca.

INTRODUCTION

The game of Patience is known to many people; though not, I would suggest, in its many variations.

To some, it conjures up the image of staid Victorian matrons of unimpeachable morals, whiling away the evenings in innocent amusement. To others, it is a game to be played by children or invalids. These views are valid, but too narrow.

Many and varied are the people who have loved the game. Napoleon, while in exile on the island of St. Helena, wrote that he passed the evenings in Patience-playing. Samuel Butler, the heretical Victorian writer, shows a softer side to his character when hunting through the British Museum Reading Room catalogues for new games to satisfy a sick friend, *his* invention and memory having been exhausted.

Tolstoy was keen to the point of obsession on playing Patience. At times he used it to decide on a course of action. (Although he was not above replaying any game that did not give the answer he wished!) He included the game in a scene from his masterpiece, *War and Peace*.

Another Russian writer, Dostoyevsky, makes his character, the siren Grushenka in *The Brothers Karamazov*, play a Russian Patience called 'Fools' at a time of great anxiety.

Today, many enjoy unwinding after a hectic day with a game that will not engender bad feeling or an empty wallet! I have even seen this being done on an InterCity train between Paddington and Bristol, not without 'help' from passers-by on their way to the buffet.

And a game that does not need a partner is a godsend to a harassed parent with a bored child with nothing to do.

As with most card games, its origins are obscure. In America it is called Solitaire, the reason for this being obvious; the British favoured the name Patience, that being the virtue nurtured in the successful ending of a game.

It was not until the nineteenth century that books began to appear, listing the many games of Patience and their variants. Lady Mary Cadogan compiled the first book on the subject in English, in 1870. This was taken from French sources, as is shown by the titles of the games demonstrated: *Les Quatre Coin*, *La Fortresse*, *Les Quatorze*, *Le Cadran* and others. It would be interesting to know if any were devised by Napoleon and if it was he who made the game fashionable in France.

A great populariser of the game in the 1890's was Miss Whitmore Jones, whose volumes went from reprint to reprint for thirty years.

I come to the end of this brief comment on the game. But take heed: Patience does not *always* possess a calming quality. The frustration of a very complicated game which 'comes out' only once in ten or twenty attempts, or of the simpler *Clock Patience* being brought to a sickeningly abrupt termination by dealing oneself four kings in a row — after which one cannot even begin — has to be felt to be believed!

Still, a successful conclusion is all the more satisfying after these. So then, let us begin ...

All Patience games are played with a standard pack of fifty-two cards, the jokers are not included.

There are four suits in each pack (clubs, diamonds, hearts and spades), the sequence running ace, two, three, four, five, six, seven, eight, nine, ten, jack (also known as 'knave'), queen and king. The latter three cards are called the 'court cards'.

When the court cards need a numerical value, the jack is valued at eleven, the queen at twelve and the king at thirteen. The ace always has a *numerical* value of one.

A 'piquet' pack is the name given to an ordinary pack with all cards below seven removed, but retaining the ace.

'Foundation' cards are the all-important base cards of the piles, on which are to be built the entire pack (or packs) in the required order. The aces often take this role, but not always.

The 'tableau' consists of cards arranged upon the table at the beginning of a game in the way the game dictates. One usually builds downwards upon an available or exposed card here until it is possible to remove them to foundation piles. A successful game will find *all* tableau cards transferred thus.

The 'reserve' holds cards on which *no* building takes place, ever!

To 'build up in suit' means to place the two of one suit onto the ace of the same suit, the three of that suit onto the two, the four onto the three, and so on, all the way to the king of that suit.

To 'play regardless of suit' is to look only at the number of the card, ignoring whether the card is a club, diamond, heart or spade, so that you play any three on any two, any four on any three, etc.

The 'heap' or 'heaps' contain the cards which cannot be played at that moment, but will be brought back into play as soon as is possible. All cards in the heap face upwards, but only the top card is available for use. There must be no rummaging through the heap for the card needed, useful as it would be on countless occasions!

It is important always to shuffle the cards thoroughly between games.

If you have known these simple rules from the cradle, I can do nothing but apologise.

1

INFURIATINGLY SIMPLE?

This small group differs from most Patience games. Here, the cards' sole purpose in life is to eliminate each other: rather like a job description for Chicago gangsters in the nineteen-twenties.

(Beware: these games can become strangely addictive.)

ROLL-CALL PATIENCE

The *Roll-Call Patience* is the simplest game of all, with absolutely no skill required. I have included it here because children love it and feel grown-up in playing it. It can also help them to count and recognise shapes. One pack is needed.

Remove all cards below seven, but retain the aces. (This is sometimes called a piquet pack.) Shuffle, then deal out the cards face upwards, one upon another, saying as you do so: seven, eight, nine, ten, jack, queen, king, ace. If a card of the right number turns up, put it to one side.

Once you have dealt out all the cards, deal them out again but don't start each new deal counting from seven; just follow on from the last number called out. Continue playing until either: (a) all the cards have answered correctly to the roll-call or (b) you find that you can remove no more and the cards always come round in the same order. If *this* happens, you have failed in your attempt.

N.B. Children tend to continue this until stopped by the removal of the cards by an adult, who considers two hours quite sufficient!

THE BARONESS PATIENCE

One pack of cards, with the four kings removed, is needed for this.

Simple this elderly Patience may be, but it is addictive. Try it.

Deal out a row of five cards from left to right, face upwards.

Remove any two cards which total thirteen when added together, such as ace and queen, seven and six, five and eight and so on. (Now you understand why the kings, valued at thirteen, are removed before the start of play.) Do look closely at the cards which remain: there may be more pairs adding up to the number required.

Deal another row of five cards across spaces or cards not taken away and play as before.

Continue this until all the cards in your hand have been dealt. (The final row will contain eight cards.)

A successful game will have all the cards paired and removed from the board.

NUMBER ELEVEN PATIENCE

Only one pack is needed for this game. Place twelve piles of four cards each, in three rows, only the top cards being placed face up. The last four are kept as a reserve as shown.

Remove any two cards that add up to eleven. The court cards have no number value and can only be taken away when any king, queen and jack are displayed at the same time.

When you have found all the available elevens, there will be piles face down; turn the top cards of these face up and look for the number eleven, in two cards, as before. As the piles become exhausted, fill the vacant space with a card taken from the four in reserve.

If you do not succeed in removing all the cards, you have failed.

Fig. 1. Number Eleven Patience.
The king of clubs, the queen of diamonds and the jack of clubs can be removed as they are there *simultaneously*. (Suit is of no importance.) The remaining queen will have to wait for another king and jack to surface.

The eight of spades and three of hearts, the seven of clubs and the four of hearts, together with the nine of diamonds and two of diamonds, can be taken away as each pair totals eleven.

PAIRS PATIENCE

This is a very simple Patience, but addictive in as much that one tends to want to play on until successful!

Only one pack is required and it is vital that this is well shuffled. Place nine cards in three rows of three, facing upwards. Remove any pairs that there may be and fill the vacant spaces from the pack. (See fig. 2 overleaf.)

If you come to a stop, you may take one card from the pack in your hand and lay it down. This usually gets the game moving again, and can be done as often as is needed.

Should this card *not* find a pair, the game has failed.

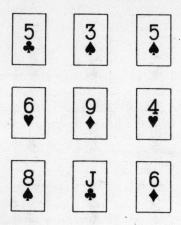

Fig. 2. Pairs Patience.
There are two pairs to be removed.

TRIPLETS PATIENCE

One pack of cards is necessary for this venerable Patience. All cards face upwards.

Deal sixteen groups of three cards, each trio overlapping one another in the shape of a fan. Four cards remain: use these to make two fans of two.

The aim of the game is not to build on a foundation, but to eliminate all cards in numerical groups of three, ignoring suit, until just one card remains. (For example: five, six, seven; or queen, king, ace; or king, ace, two; or nine, ten, jack.)

Only the exposed card at the top of each fan, that with nothing upon it, is available for play and each card removed must be taken from a different fan. It is not permitted to dispose of an original fan in one fell swoop!

Some, of more heroic stature, make the game more difficult by removing one card from the pack before the game begins and attempt to empty the table completely.

PUSH-PIN PATIENCE

Two packs are needed for this very simple Patience. Shuffle the packs together very thoroughly, then deal out the cards from left to right and side by side, face upwards.

Whenever one or two cards are between two others of the same value or suit, discard them and close ranks. (Seven of clubs and three of diamonds between the queen of hearts and the queen of spades, discard the seven and three. Eight of hearts and two of spades between the five of diamonds and the jack of diamonds, discard the eight and two.)

Should there be three or *more* cards caught in this way, all can be removed *only* if they are of the same suit. (Queen, ten, six, three and two of diamonds imprisoned between the four of clubs and jack of clubs, take away all the diamonds.)

The game is won if two cards remain side by side at the end, all the others having been taken away.

(There is a second chance, however, if a line of whatever length remains when all the cards have been played out. Switch any two cards in the row to revive the game.)

DRIVEL PATIENCE

You will need one pack of cards for this game. It is a simple Patience, but I think the alternative title, *Idiot's Delight*, is going too far.

Shuffle the pack very thoroughly and deal four cards in a row, face upwards.

If any of the cards are of the same suit, remove those of a lower value and put them to one side. The highest card in that suit remains in its place. (Aces are of a higher value than kings in this game.)

Fill the gap, or gaps, with the next card from those held in your hand. Should *that* card be lower than another in the same suit on the table, remove that, too.

Continue until you have four cards of a different suit, then deal out four cards at a time on top of the previous four, discarding all the lower value cards in the same suit as before.

Gaps made by the removal of all the cards in a pile must be filled *at once* with the top card from one of the three other piles. This releases the card beneath, hopefully for removal. It is wise to play an ace into a gap whenever possible.

A successful conclusion to the game sees the four aces in a row, all the other cards of lower value having been removed.

NARCOTIC PATIENCE

You will need one pack of cards for this Patience. I think the title of this game highly inappropriate. It does *not* soothe. On the contrary, it goads one until nothing is more important than to bring it to a successful end!

Shuffle the cards very well and deal four cards in a row, face upwards. If there are two of the same value, place the card on the right onto the card on the left. (The same rule applies if there are three of the same value. The duplicates are always piled upon the card of the same value to the left.)

Continue dealing four cards at a time on top of the previous four, pausing between each deal to move those of equal rank to the leftmost card.

All the cards in your hand having been used, gather up the piles from right to left, without reshuffling or disturbing their order in any way, and deal them out again (and again and again!). There is no limit to the times this can be done.

Should the four cards you deal have the same value, remove them from the game. The Patience is won when all fifty-two cards have been taken away in this way.

I refuse to say how long this took me, but I will admit to more than one hour ...

2

A LITTLE CO-OPERATION
GOES A LONG WAY

In sampling this selection you will have to play both carefully *and* with the full co-operation of the cards — not often given!

✓ AULD LANG SYNE PATIENCE

You will need one pack of cards for this game. Take the four aces from the pack and place them in a row, face upwards.

The object of the game is to build on these aces, or foundations, in sequence and in suit up to the king.

Shuffle the pack thoroughly and deal out four cards, face upwards, in a row below the foundation cards. Stop to see whether any card can be used (two of diamonds onto ace of diamonds, for example), then place a further four cards upon those dealt previously, or onto the gaps if you *have* been fortunate enough to be able to use them.

Continue to lay down four cards at a time, building on the foundations after each deal whenever possible. A card having been removed enables the exposed card beneath to be used, too.

No redeal is permitted. The four foundation piles must be crowned with their kings, or the game is lost.

A variant to this game, entitled *Tam O'Shanter*, will not permit the aces to be removed first. One has to wait until they emerge in the course of play! 'Had we but world enough, and time ...'

CLOCK PATIENCE

Only one pack of cards is needed for this. Shuffle the cards thoroughly, then deal out, face down, twelve cards in the shape of a clock face. Place a thirteenth card in the centre, also face down.

Repeat this until you have thirteen piles of four cards, then turn the top card on the thirteenth pile face up. If, for example, this is the five of diamonds, place it face up underneath the five o'clock pile on your clock face. Leave it protruding somewhat so that its number can be seen. Take the top card from the five o'clock pile and put it under its appropriate number pile.

An ace is placed at one o'clock, a jack at eleven o'clock and a queen at twelve o'clock. A king is placed under the pile in the middle.

The object of the game is to have all the cards face up in the right piles, but this happens rarely because once all the kings have turned up it is impossible to continue.

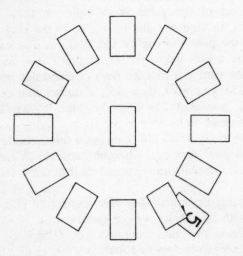

Fig. 3. Clock Patience.

GRANDFATHER'S CLOCK PATIENCE

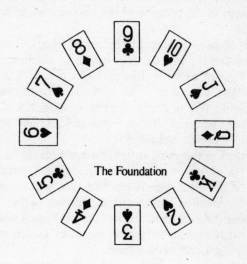

The Foundation

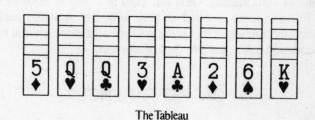

The Tableau

Fig. 4. Grandfather's Clock Patience.
A good beginning – the five of diamonds, three of hearts *and* ace of clubs can be removed to their respective foundation piles, immediately freeing the cards above them for use. (All cards face upwards.)

One pack of cards is needed for this Patience. The twelve foundation cards — see below — are set out in a circle before play begins. (All cards must face upwards in this game.)

Remove the following to be used as the foundation cards, putting them in the position of the corresponding hour on the clock face:

Nine of clubs — twelve o'clock; ten of hearts — one o'clock; jack of spades — two o'clock; queen of diamonds — three o'clock; king of clubs — four o'clock; two of hearts — five o'clock; three of spades — six o'clock; four of diamonds — seven o'clock; five of clubs — eight o'clock; six of hearts — nine o'clock; seven of spades — ten o'clock; and the eight of diamonds — eleven o'clock.

The object of the game is to build upwards on each card, in suit and in sequence, until the appropriate number to its position on the clock face is reached. You will remember that the jack is valued at eleven and the queen, twelve.

After shuffling the remainder of the pack, deal out five rows of eight cards each, overlapping the rows so that the tableau resembles eight vertical columns.

The exposed, or available, card at the base of each column can be played to a foundation pile, if at all possible, or used to build downwards in sequence, but ignoring suit, on another column until needed. Only one card at a time is to be moved.

Fill a column emptied in play with any available card. A successful ending to this game will see all cards gathered to the foundation piles and the 'hours' correct.

CARPET PATIENCE

This simple Patience requires one pack of cards. Place upon the table four rows of five cards each, all facing upwards. This forms the 'carpet' of the title.

As the aces emerge, put two to the right and two to the left of the carpet.

Build up on the aces, in suit, to their respective king. Any of the cards in the carpet are available for use. Use the cards in your hand to build on the aces or to form a single heap of those not immediately playable. As always, the top card of the heap is available.

As 'holes' are made in the carpet, fill the gaps with cards from the heap or from those in your hand.

It is not permitted to gather up and replay the heap, neither is this often necessary.

PERPETUAL MOTION PATIENCE

Never was a game so well named. It is also addictive to a maddening degree.

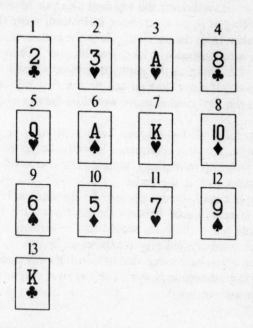

Fig. 5. Perpetual Motion Patience.
The nine of spades will move to beneath the two of clubs, missing the correctly placed king of clubs.

You will need one pack, well shuffled. Begin by dealing out, face upwards, thirteen piles of four cards. Imagine that these piles are numbered from one to thirteen and line them up in whatever way helps you to remember. (As usual, the jack equals eleven, the queen twelve and the king has the value of thirteen.)

The object of the game is to eliminate the pack, in batches of thirteen, in the following way.

Take the top card from the pile numbered one, putting it beneath pile number two. Move the top card from pile number two to the bottom of pile number three, continuing in this way until you arrive at pile number thirteen. The top card from *this* pile returns to the bottom of pile number one. (The *Perpetual Motion* of the title.)

However, whenever the top card of a pile agrees with your numbering of it, do not remove it. Instead, move the card you have taken from the previous pile to the bottom of the next pile which is *not* topped with its correct number. (There will be less and less of these as the game progresses.) Going back to the beginning, if there was an ace on the first pile as the game began, the first card to move would be the top of pile number two.

Hopefully, all top thirteen cards will soon be where they should be, running in sequence from the ace to the king. Then is the time to remove them, putting them to one side. They take no further part in the game.

The last card removed before the thirteen cards were taken away is now placed beneath the next pile to it (or the next available under the rules should that be already topped by its correct number) and play continues as before.

Should you have succeeded in spiriting away three sequences of thirteen, the game is won. The last layer will be correct, but do not ask me how!

SPOILT PATIENCE

Again, a very simple Patience, but none the worse for that!

One pack of cards is required, with all the twos, threes, fours, fives and sixes removed. (This is sometimes called a piquet pack.)

Lay out four rows of seven cards each, facing downwards, with a reserve of four cards placed to one side, also face down.

The four rows represent four different suits in the following order: first diamonds, second hearts, third clubs and the fourth row is spades.

Take the first card in the reserve and put it in its correct place, face up. If it is an ace it will be first in its own row, if a king the second, if a ten the fifth and so on.

(Let us assume that the first card in the reserve is the jack of clubs. Lift the concealed card that is lying in the place where the jack of clubs *should* be and lay the jack there. Put the card thus ousted into the correct place for *it*, removing the card that is lying there. Play on in the same way, placing and removing.)

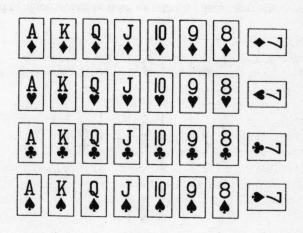

Fig. 6. A successful Spoilt Patience.

Should you discover a seven while doing this, for which there is no space available, place it horizontally at the end of the appropriate row and take a card from the reserve to continue the game.

If you turn over the *fourth* seven while there are still cards face down, there is one last chance to make the game a success. Turn one of the remaining concealed cards and, if it is in the correct place, lay it down face up and turn another. This enables you to play on.

The game has failed if the card chosen was not where it should be: a *Spoilt Patience*.

CZARINA PATIENCE

One pack of cards (well shuffled) is needed for this game.

Deal five cards on to the table, face upwards and in the shape of a cross; this is the tableau. The next card from those you hold is put, face up, into the left-hand corner. This is the first foundation card. Three other cards of the same value must be placed in the remaining corners, as soon as they emerge in play.

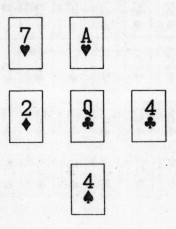

Fig. 7. Czarina Patience.
The first foundation card has been placed.

The object of the game is to build a thirteen card sequence, upwards and in suit, on each foundation. (Fig. 7 has the seven of hearts as an example. Thus, the sequence will run seven, eight, nine, ten, jack, queen, king, ace, two, three, four, five and end with a six.) To achieve this, you will be building *downwards*, regardless of suit, onto the cross cards until these cards can be removed to a foundation pile.

Build any cards that can be used from the tableau onto the foundations, filling gaps from those you hold. (Later in the game, a gap may be filled with *any* card available; that is, the top card of the heap, of a tableau pile or those in your hand.)

If, in the initial tableau, you are fortunate enough to deal consecutively numbered cards, for example, a jack *and* a queen, you can build down immediately by placing the jack on top of the queen. Then another card can be dealt into the space that is left. This rarely happens if the cards are well shuffled.

Now begin to deal your cards, one by one. Play them upwards onto the foundations, or downwards onto the cross cards until needed. Unplayable cards are put face up onto a single heap and, yes, the top of this is always available for you to use!

When all the cards have been used, no redeal of the heap is permitted.

The game has succeeded if each foundation pile contains thirteen cards, built upwards in suit, causing the central cross to vanish silently away.

KNAVES' DIAL PATIENCE

This is one of the more simple games, requiring two packs of cards, for days when only a gentle brainteaser is needed. This does *not* mean that a happy ending is automatic.

Begin by shuffling the two packs together, very thoroughly. Turn the top card – this will decide the suit of the twelve foundations.

Excluding the jack (or knave), arrange the cards of this suit in a semicircle, as they emerge in play, running from the ace to the king. All cards face upwards.

The eight jacks play no part in this game. They are placed in two rows of four, inside the half circle or 'dial'.

The object of the game is to build the other seven cards, of the same value, upon each of the corresponding cards in the semicircle, alternating the colours. (The suit being diamonds, a black ace will be placed on the ace of diamonds, a red ace on the black ace and so on.) But you need *all* the foundation cards in place *before* you can put any cards of the opposing colour on top of them.

Deal out the cards in your hand one by one. If possible, play these upon the foundation cards or discard them to a single heap, the top of which remains available, as ever.

All cards having been used, turn over the heap and play it

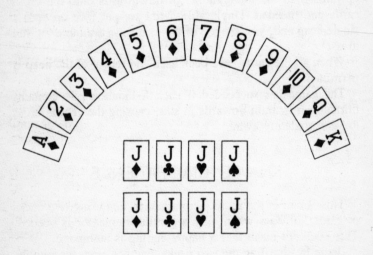

Fig. 8. Knaves' Dial Patience.
In this game, the ten of diamonds was the top card.

through again, once. If you have been successful, the dial will have changed colour; in *this* game from red to black.

PAS SEUL PATIENCE

One pack of cards is needed for this. *Pas Seul*, peering back through the mists of time to ballet classes, is that golden opportunity yearned for by budding Pavlovas, the solo-dance. A most suitable title for a Patience.

All cards in this game face upwards. Begin by dealing out six cards in a row for the tableau.

Your object is to take the aces as they emerge in play, building upwards upon them in suit and sequence to the king. (Put these foundation cards, when discovered, in a line at the top of the table.)

Start by removing any aces, and cards that can be built upon them, from the tableau. Fill the resulting gaps, if any, with cards taken from those you hold.

If your tableau consists of consecutively numbered cards of alternating colours (e.g. a red seven and a black eight), build these cards downwards on each other (e.g. place the red seven onto the black eight). Again, fill any resulting gaps with cards taken from those you hold.

After this, deal out the pack one by one. Build on the foundation piles wherever possible or build downwards on the tableau cards, in sequence but alternating the colours, until they can be removed. Overlap these cards to make six columns of differing lengths.

Discard unplayable cards to a single heap. Cards available for you to use are the top card of the heap (naturally), the top card of those in your hand, the exposed card at the base of a column or any part of a downward sequence, provided that the rule about alternating colours is observed. This is very useful in extricating a vital card.

Gaps in the tableau, a column having been played off, are filled by any one available card *or* a sequence.

No second chance is given in this game as one may not redeal the heap.

PYRAMID PATIENCE

One pack of cards is needed for this simple Patience. Shuffle the pack thoroughly (absolutely vital in this game) and construct a pyramid in the following fashion.

Deal out, face upwards, five rows of cards as a reserve in the shape of a pyramid: one card in the top row, two in the second, three in the third, four in the fourth and five cards in the bottom row.

The object of the game is to remove the four aces, as they surface in play, to the top of the table, building upwards upon each in sequence and in suit to the king.

Every card in the reserve is available for use. Take away from there any aces, and cards to be built on them, filling spaces from the cards you hold.

Now deal your cards one by one, either to a foundation pile or to a single heap, remembering that the top of this yearns to be of assistance.

No redeal of the heap is permitted when all your cards are played.

A successful ending will find the pyramid vanished and four neat piles, each crowned with a king.

LES QUATORZE PATIENCE

Two packs of cards are needed for this game. Shuffle the cards and deal out twenty-five cards, face upwards, in five rows, each containing five cards. The object of this Patience is to make the number fourteen with any two cards, taken only from a perpendicular or from a horizontal row. The cards paired in this way are placed to one side and their places taken by the cards in your hand.

The jack counts as eleven, the queen twelve and the king thirteen.

If, during the game, the number fourteen cannot be made, one has a second chance. Any two cards may be taken from their proper position and may change places with two other cards so as to make one or more fourteens. This exchange of cards can be done only once in each playing.

If you are successful in this game, the entire pack will be paired off.

In the example given, the queen of diamonds can be paired with the two of spades, the king of hearts with the ace of clubs, the jack of hearts with the three of diamonds and the six of spades with the eight of hearts.

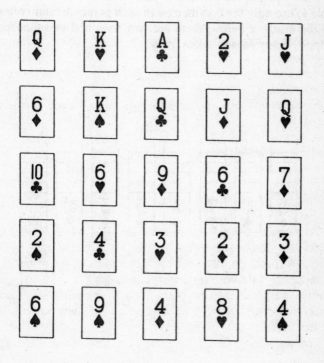

Fig. 9. Les Quatorze Patience.

MATRIMONY PATIENCE

For this game, one pack is required. Shuffle the cards very thoroughly, then place forty-eight cards, face up, in six rows of eight cards each. If, as you deal out the cards, you find two cards of equal value (such as two fours or two jacks, etc.) in the same perpendicular column, do not lay the second card down. Put it at the bottom of the pack in your hand and substitute the next. The four cards remaining are the reserve and should be put to one side face down. The success of the game depends on them.

The object of the game is to pair off all the cards, but being able to use only the bottom card in each perpendicular column. In the example below, there are two fives and two tens to be happily married and taken away.

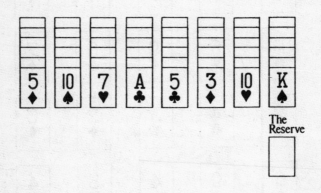

Fig. 10. Matrimony Patience.
The Layout. (All cards, except those in the reserve, are placed face up.)

Their departing will uncover other cards and *may* enable other pairs to be made. If this is not the case, and the game is at a standstill, take the top reserve card and try to set the game moving again. When the reserve pile is exhausted, if all the couples are not married, the game has failed.

PICTURE PATIENCE

You will need two packs of cards for this game, but do not shuffle the packs together.

To begin, take one pack and lay out nine cards in three rows (three cards in each row), facing upwards. Then play out the cards in your hand into a heap; placing the four aces, as they appear, in a perpendicular line on the left. The four kings, as

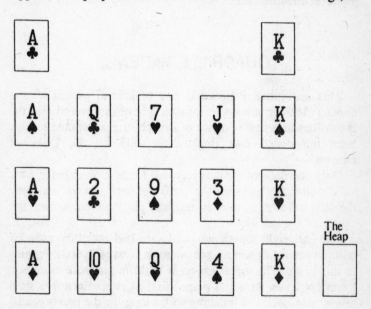

Fig. 11. Picture Patience — ready to begin.
(All cards face upwards.)

they appear, are placed to the right. The aces are built on upwards, in suit. (Two of hearts to be placed on the ace of hearts, three of hearts to be placed on the two and so on.) The final card on these piles will be a king.

The kings are built on downwards, in suit. (Queen of hearts to be placed on the king of hearts, jack of hearts to be placed on the queen and so on.) The final card on these piles, if successfully worked out, will be an ace.

Whenever you can use a card from the centre nine, replace it with the top card from the heap. When you have worked your way through the first pack, continue with the second. The aces and kings from this pack are put on the waste heap or become one of the nine central cards until they can be correctly placed. The heap can be turned over when all the cards are used, and played through once again to give one a second chance. If all the cards are not placed in their proper sequence after this, the game is unsuccessful.

QUADRILLE PATIENCE

This decorative Patience is one of several named after a dance. (Seeking always to inform, I have discovered that the quadrille was a square dance of French origin, reputed to have been introduced into England in 1813 by the Duke of Devonshire!)

Only one pack of cards is required for this. Shuffle the pack very thoroughly and deal the cards out onto a heap, removing the aces and twos as they emerge and placing them to form the figure of a quadrille.

Once all eight foundation cards are laid out, they must be built on according to suit, but not as in most of the other games in this book. This time you must build in alternate numbers: for example, on the ace is placed first a three, next a five, then seven, nine, jack and finishing with a king; on the two is placed a four, then a six, followed by eight, ten and finishing with a queen.

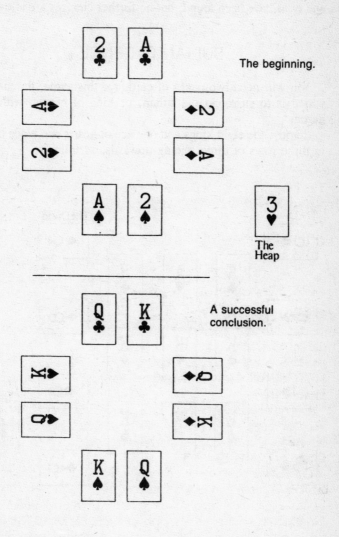

Fig. 12. Quadrille Patience.

There is only one heap, so progress can be very difficult sometimes. The heap can be used twice more after all the aces and twos have been found, but no further chances are allowed.

SULTAN PATIENCE

You will need two packs of cards for this game, the aim of which is to surround the sultan, or king of hearts, with his harem.

Remove the eight kings and one ace of hearts and place them in three rows of three, facing upwards, as follows:

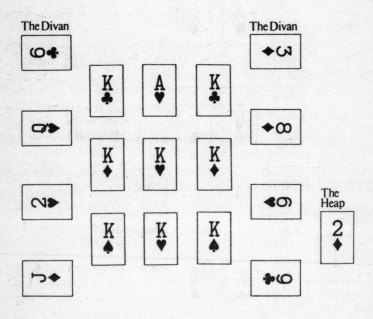

Fig. 13. Sultan Patience – ready to begin.

Top row: king of clubs, ace of hearts, king of clubs.
Middle row: king of diamonds, king of hearts (the
                sultan), king of diamonds.
Bottom row: king of spades, king of hearts and king of
                spades.

Give the rest of the cards a good shuffle, then deal out eight cards and place them face upwards at right angles, four to the left and four to the right of the square. These cards are called the 'divan', the Turkish word for a long bench covered in cushions, much in evidence in Victorian paintings of the mysterious harem.

The king of hearts in the centre is not to be covered by any other card. The other kings and the ace of hearts are to be built in suit up to their respective queen. (The ace is placed on the king, the two on the ace, etc. The two of hearts is placed upon the ace of hearts and so on.)

Use the cards in your hand to build if possible, or place them onto a single heap, the top card of which is always available.

When there is a suitable card in the divan, this must be used and the space filled from the top of the heap. (If there is no heap at that moment, use the next card from those you hold in your hand.)

All the cards having been used, the heap may be played twice *without reshuffling*.

If the game has come out successfully, the king of hearts is to be seen surrounded by his eight queens.

ALHAMBRA PATIENCE

You will need two packs of cards for this game, somewhat strangely named after the citadel and palace in Granada, built at the behest of the Moorish kings of the thirteenth century.

Remove the ace and the king of each suit from one pack, putting these eight cards at the top of the table as foundation cards.

The aim of the game is to build the aces up in sequence and in suit to the king (ace, two, three, four, five, six, seven, eight, nine, ten, jack, queen and king). The kings build downwards in sequence and suit to the ace.

Shuffle the remaining cards together very thoroughly and deal out a reserve of four rows of eight cards each, face upwards, from left to right. Overlap the rows so that the layout resembles eight upright columns, with the value of each card clearly seen.

Use any suitable exposed card (those at the base of a column with nothing upon them) to build on the foundation cards. By doing this you release the cards above for use.

When you can do no more, play out the cards in your hand one by one, building up or down wherever possible.

There is no building on the reserve. Discard useless cards to a single heap, the use of which is somewhat different from the norm. Exposed cards in the reserve can be played to the top of the heap, if their numbering is consecutive, either up or down. Suit is of no importance. For example, if the card on the top of the heap is a seven, an exposed card valued at six or eight can be moved on to it. This is very useful in unblocking trapped cards, as you will appreciate!

The heap can be turned over and played through again twice at the end of the first deal, but careful planning is needed for a successful conclusion.

A *horrible* variation of this Patience begins with the reserve dealt out in eight piles of four cards, with only the top card facing upwards. I believe this to be impossible to bring out. (Well, I can't do it …)

CAPTIVE QUEENS PATIENCE

One pack of cards is required for this game. Remove the four queens from the pack and place them face upwards, one upon another, in the centre of the table. These are the 'captive queens'.

All the fives and all the sixes are arranged in a circle around the queens, also facing upwards. Once the opening tableau has been arranged, the Patience is ready to begin.

The fives and the sixes are the foundation cards. The object of the game is to build upwards on the sixes, in suit, to the jacks and to build downwards, in suit, on the fives to the kings. (This last runs five, four, three, two, ace, king.)

Using the cards in your hand, build on the foundation cards if possible. Place those not immediately needed face upwards on a single heap. The top card is always available for use.

You are permitted to replay the heap once, but there must be no reshuffling of the cards, however useful this might be to a happy ending!

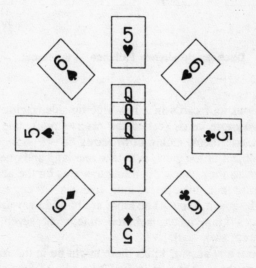

Fig. 14. Captive Queens Patience – ready to begin.

DUCHESS DE LUYNES PATIENCE

You will need two packs of cards for this game.

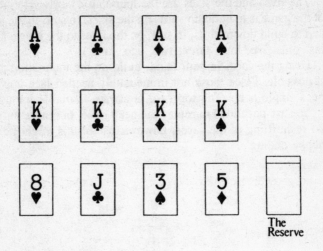

Fig. 15.   Duchess de Luynes Patience — the layout.

Deal out four cards in a row side by side, facing upwards, with two more cards (called the reserve pile), one upon the other beside them, facing downwards.

The object of the game is to take one king and one ace from each suit as they appear, building upwards on the aces, in suit to the king (ace, two, three, four, five, six, seven, eight, nine, ten, jack, queen, king). The kings are built downwards, in suit to the aces (king, queen, jack, ten, nine, eight, seven, six, five, four, three, two, ace).

Remove any aces or kings there might be in the row of four and place them as shown in fig. 15; a row of four aces at the top and a row of four kings in the middle are required.

Continue dealing four cards onto the previous four and two cards onto the reserve pile. Pause between each deal to see whether there are any kings and aces to be removed or any building (up or down) that can be done.

When all the cards in your hand have been used, spread out the reserve pile and remove any cards that can be used immediately. Then check to see whether any exposed cards on the row of four can be built onto the king/ace piles. If so, build them accordingly.

After this, gather up the four piles from right to left and put the unused remnants of the reserve pile on top. Continue the game as before. Three redeals are permitted but, on the last redeal omit the reserve pile and just deal out one row of four cards.

I am told that there is a Patience game, entitled *Parisienne*, with precisely the same rules, the only difference being the removal and placing of the four kings and the four aces *before* the game begins. It makes life a little easier, I suppose ...

ROUGE ET NOIR PATIENCE

You will need two packs of cards for this game. Begin by removing the eight aces from the packs and place them side by side in a row, facing upwards.

Below these foundation cards deal out a row of eight cards, also face up and side by side. This is the tableau.

The object of the game is to build upwards, in sequence, on these ace foundation cards to the king. The difference in this game is that the piles are built in alternating colours, the red and black of the title (a red two on a black ace, a black three on a red two, and so on).

Take any suitable cards from the tableau and place them on the foundations. Fill any gaps from the cards you hold in your hand.

If you have consecutively-numbered cards in the tableau of opposing colours, you can build *downwards* on them, i.e. place a black seven on a red eight. Again, fill any gaps from the cards you hold in your hand.

Begin to play, dealing one card at a time. Anything that

cannot be placed immediately on the foundation cards can be built downwards on the tableau until needed or onto a single heap, the top card of which is always available for use.

Single cards can be moved from the top of each tableau pile onto the foundations, or from the top of one tableau pile to the top of another, if this is helpful; but never to fill a gap.

Gaps in the tableau line must be filled immediately from the top of the heap. If the heap has been used, fill the spaces with cards dealt from those you hold. Should *those* have been exhausted, the gap must remain a gap!

One redeal is permitted when all the cards have been dealt. Pick up the heap, turn it over and play on as before.

The game is won if all the foundation piles have been built in alternate colours up to the king.

LEGITIMIST PATIENCE

I remain in cheerful ignorance as to the identity of the supporter of the French royal house of Bourbon who (presumably) invented this Patience. It does not stop me playing it.

Two packs of cards are needed. Shuffle both packs together, first removing one king and placing it upon the table. (All cards are placed face upwards in this game and the suit is of no importance.)

As they emerge in play, put in a row beside the king from left to right, a queen, jack, ten, nine, eight, seven and six. These are the foundation cards (or *origines* as the French has it). There is one difficulty. Foundation cards *must* be moved into position in the order stated (the queen before the jack, eight before seven, etc.).

The object of the game is to build, in sequence, downwards on these, paying no attention to suit. Thus, in a successful game, the king finishes the thirteen card sequence topped with an ace, the queen with a king, the jack with a queen, ten with a jack, nine with a ten, eight with a nine, seven with an eight and six with a seven. But you don't have to wait until you have all the foundation cards in place before you start building.

Play the cards in your hand one by one upon any available foundation card. If they cannot be used immediately, put them in a single heap, the top card of which is always available.

The heap can be turned over and redealt twice. If you have not succeeded ... well, 'tant pis!'

QUADRUPLE ALLIANCE PATIENCE

One pack of cards is needed for this game. Ignoring suit, remove any one ace, two, three and four and put them in a row, face upwards.

Below this make a second row, consisting of any two, four, six and eight. These last four are the foundation cards.

You must aim to build upwards, still disregarding suit, on the lower row until a king tops each base. The sequences run as follows:

   (a) two, three, four, five, six, seven, eight, nine, ten, jack, queen, king.

   (b) four, six, eight, ten, queen, ace, three, five, seven, nine, jack, king.

   (c) six, nine, queen, two, five, eight, jack, ace, four, seven, ten, king.

   (d) eight, queen, three, seven, jack, two, six, ten, ace, five, nine, king.

This is not *too* complicated, if one remembers that the cards in the top row are there solely to remind the player by what amount the cards below are to advance.

Play the cards in your hand one by one. Build on a foundation if possible, otherwise discard them face up onto a single heap, the top card of which is there to be used whenever possible.

All cards dealt? Turn over the heap and play it through again twice. After this, the kings have no further chance to seal their alliance.

SQUARE PATIENCE

Two packs of cards, well shuffled together, are needed for this game.

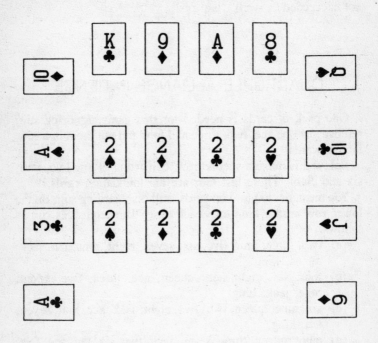

Fig. 16. Square Patience.

Deal out twelve cards, facing upwards, to make three sides of a square: four cards at the top and four at each side. This is the tableau.

Remove the twos as they emerge in play, placing them in two rows of four inside the confines of the square, face up, naturally.

The object of the game is to build upwards, in suit and sequence, until each foundation is crowned by its respective ace. (The sequence runs two, three, four, five, six, seven, eight, nine, ten, jack, queen, king and ace.)

Deal out the cards you hold in your hand one by one. Build upwards on the twos, if there are any available, or build downwards in suit on any suitable card in the tableau (e.g. onto the ace of diamonds put the king, queen, jack, ten, etc. of diamonds) until these can be played to the foundation piles. (If, when you deal out the tableau at the start of the game, you have consecutively-numbered cards in the same suit, you can, of course, build downwards on them and then deal other cards into any spaces.)

Unplayable cards are discarded face up to a single heap, the top card of which is always available. A space in the tableau, caused by the removal of a card or pile, is filled with a card taken from the top of the heap.

I hope that all the foundation piles are now topped with their aces, no second deal of the heap being allowed.

A variant to this game, named *Deuces*, is a little less difficult. All the foundation twos are put in place *before* the game begins, but the columns of the tableau to left and right have three cards in each, not four. The rest of the Patience is played in the same way, but this game *does* allow a redeal.

ODD AND EVEN PATIENCE

Two packs of cards are requisite for this Patience. Shuffle the packs together thoroughly and begin by dealing out nine cards, in three rows of three, facing upwards. These are the reserve.

Remove one ace and one two of each suit as they emerge in play. These are put in a line above the reserve, totalling eight foundation cards in all. If at the beginning of the game, you deal any aces and twos into the reserve, you can, of course, use these as foundation cards and fill the spaces left behind by them with other cards.

The object of the game is to build upwards, in suit and sequence, on both the ace and the two as follows:

Ace, three, five, seven, nine, jack, king, two, four, six, eight, ten and queen.

Two, four, six, eight, ten, queen, ace, three, five, seven, nine, jack, king.

In this way, the title is justified!

Begin to deal the cards in your hand one by one, building on the foundation piles whenever possible. Cards not playable for the moment are discarded to a single heap, the top card of this being always available.

Use the cards in the reserve whenever you can. A space (or spaces) here must be filled immediately with the top card from the heap. (Should this have vanished away or not yet begun, use the next card from those you hold.)

Turn over the heap and play it through once again (and once only) when all cards have been dealt.

HERRING-BONE PATIENCE

I have a weakness for the more colourful layouts: this is one such, and the title is appropriate. Two packs are needed.

After shuffling the packs together, deal out two rows of three cards as a tableau, one above the other. (All cards in this Patience face upwards.)

If a jack is among the original six, remove it to the centre of the table, replacing it with the next card from the pack.

Put *all* the jacks, as they emerge in play, into the centre of the table to form a non-overlapping, upright column of eight. These are the foundation cards.

The aim of the game is to build downwards, in sequence and in suit, upon the jacks to the ace (jack, ten, nine, eight, seven, six, five, four, three, two and ace).

The king and the queen are of no value in this game, other than to add verisimilitude to the title. When a jack is in place, the king and queen of matching suit are put at an angle on either side of it; the 'herring-bone' takes shape in this way.

The royal couple must not be placed before their jack emerges, being discarded to the solitary heap or remaining in

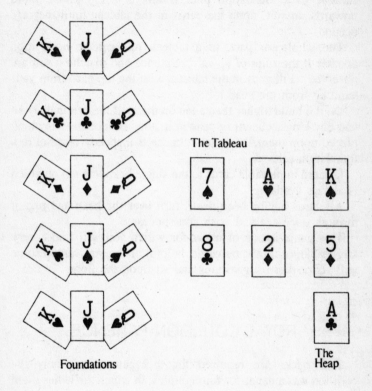

The Tableau

Foundations

The Heap

Fig. 17. Herring-Bone Patience.
A demonstration of the layout, with three jacks still to emerge.

Nothing can be built upon the king of spades in the tableau; he awaits the arrival of the second jack of spades for his removal.

waiting upon the tableau, if they arrive at the wrong time.

It is not necessary to have both king *and* queen before moving them into place.

Deal out the cards in your hand one by one. Play anything suitable to a foundation pile. If this is not possible, build upwards, in suit, upon the cards in the tableau until they are needed.

The whole, or part, of a tableau pile can be built upon another if the rules of upward sequence and matching suit are observed. (Fill gaps in the tableau with the top card from your hand or from the heap.)

Do not build higher than a ten on these. If the original layout had any kings, queens or tens in it, they cannot have anything placed upon them. Your only chance is a speedy removal to a foundation pile.

Discard unplayable cards to the single heap, the top of which is always available.

All cards having been dealt, turn over the heap and play it through once again. I wish you success.

This game is one of many for which you will find a very large table, or miniature cards, helpful. The more venturesome will scorn these suggestions and sit upon the floor.

ROYAL COTILLION PATIENCE

Two packs are required for this game. Originally the cotillion was a dance for four couples, in which the ladies lifted their skirts to reveal an inch or so of ornate petticoat (*cotillon* in French). Later the name was given to a fast waltz.

Shuffle the two packs together very thoroughly and deal out, face upwards and not overlapping, twelve cards, in three rows of four, to the left of the board. (The 'left wing'.)

Next deal sixteen cards in four rows of four to the right of the board — yes, the 'right wing'. These cards also do not overlap and all face upwards.

Between these wings, as they surface in play, are placed the

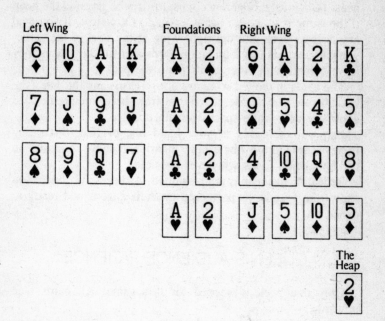

Fig. 18. Royal Cotillion Patience.
A demonstration of the layout.

foundation cards in two upright columns of four, comprising one ace and one two from each suit.

The aim of the game is to build upwards, in suit, on these foundations by two. Each thirteen card sequence runs as follows:

Ace, three, five, seven, nine, jack, king, two, four, six, eight, ten and queen.

Two, four, six, eight, ten, queen, ace, three, five, seven, nine, jack and king.

All the cards on the right wing are available for building onto the foundation piles, gaps being filled by the next card from those you hold or from the top of the, as yet unformed, solitary heap. (Obviously, preference must *always* be given to the heap if the game is to have a happy ending.) Of course, if you deal any aces or twos into the right wing at the start of the game, you can use these as foundation cards and fill the spaces they leave behind with other cards from the pack.

The cards in the left wing are not so easily caught. Only the bottom row is available, a removal from here freeing the card above for use, while spaces remain unfilled.

Play out the cards in your hand one by one, discarding useless cards to the single heap mentioned above, building on the foundation cards whenever possible.

Redealing the heap is not permitted. A successful conclusion shows the four kings partnered by their queens and ready to dance.

QUEEN'S AUDIENCE PATIENCE

Only one pack is needed for this game. All cards face upwards.

After shuffling the pack, deal out sixteen cards in the shape of a square, four to each side. The space enclosed is called the 'audience chamber', the sixteen cards the 'ante-chamber'.

The aim of the game is to move the ace and jack of each suit into the audience chamber as they emerge in play, to build downwards upon them in sequence and suit to the twos (jack, ten, nine, eight, seven, six, five, four, three and two). The ace is hidden beneath its jack and plays no further part in the game. An annoying rule dictates that both jack and ace of the same suit must be *simultaneously* available before taking up their position as a foundation pile.

Play out the cards in your hand one by one, hopefully onto a foundation pile, while discarding useless cards to a single heap, the top of which is there to be used at any time.

All the cards of the ante-chamber can be moved to the foundation piles for building when possible. Spaces made here must be filled with the top card from the heap; if there is no heap, use the next card from those you hold in your hand.

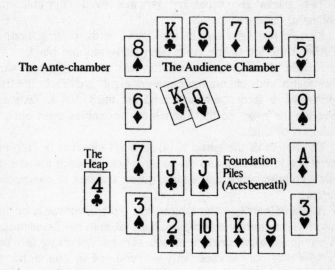

Fig. 19. Queen's Audience Patience.
Two more foundation piles are still to be found.

The ace of diamonds must remain in the ante-chamber until the jack of diamonds emerges.

The kings of clubs and diamonds await their consorts before removal to the audience chamber.

The kings and queens play a decorative role. The regal couple (same suit, naturally) are put together above a foundation pile in the audience chamber. Place the queen on top of the king to illustrate the title of the game. As before, *both* must be available at the same time before removing.

There is no redeal of the heap. A successful game has caused the ante-chamber to vanish into the four piles which remain, topped by a two.

OCTAVE PATIENCE

Two packs are necessary for this most enjoyable and colourful Patience.

Remove the eight aces as foundation cards, putting them in a row at the top of the table, alternately red and black.

Shuffle the remainder of the two packs together very thoroughly and deal out three rows of eight cards each; the first two rows to face downwards and the third row to face up. Overlap the rows, so that the tableau resembles eight upright columns of three.

The object of the game is (a) to build upwards *in suit* and sequence to the tens and (b) to have beneath each foundation pile a column containing a king, queen and jack in *alternating colours*.

Available cards in the tableau are built downwards on the columns, in alternating colours, until taken to the foundations. When an exposed card is removed, turn the one above face up.

Now play out the cards in your hand one by one, either to a foundation pile or onto the tableau (remembering the colour rule). Discard unplayable cards to a single heap, the top of which is always available.

(Only one card at a time, not a sequence, can be moved about the layout.)

Fill a column, emptied in play, with any available card, but beware: remembering the second objective, it is wiser to put a king at the top of an empty column, where possible.

Having played all the cards in your hand, gather up the heap and turn it over. A second chance is given. Deal out eight cards in a line below the tableau. Use any of these eight cards for building on the foundation piles or tableau, filling up spaces with the next card from the heap.

When none of the eight can be placed, the game is practically at an end, *but* the anonymous inventor permits a last, desperate fling. Play the next card from the heap to see if this will reanimate the game. After this, you have no more chances of ending successfully (but I trust you already have).

WHEAT-EAR PATIENCE

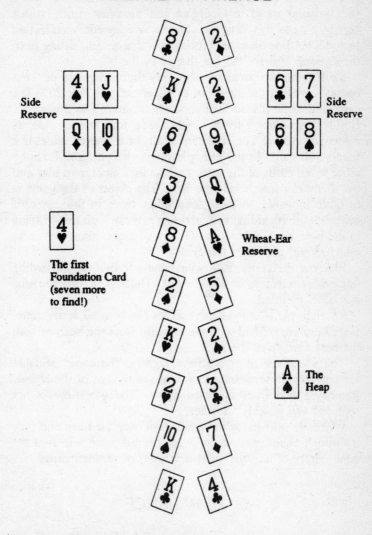

Fig. 20. Wheat-Ear Patience.
The four of spades, from the side reserve, and the four of clubs, at the base of the wheat-ear, can be removed to the foundation row immediately.

Two packs are needed for this game. The wheat-ear was a very popular motif in Georgian and Victorian times, which certainly dates this Patience. The Crown jewellery collection includes six fine diamond brooches of this design, dating from the days of William IV; but that is by the by.

Shuffle the two packs together very thoroughly and deal out twenty cards in the shape of a wheat-ear (see fig. 20). The cards are to be placed face upwards, as are all in this game. Beside them place a further eight cards, four to each side, as a second reserve. The next card dealt, of whatever value, is a foundation card. In the example given, it is a four. Take the other seven cards of the same rank as they emerge in play and put them in a row beside the first. The object of the game is to build upwards on these foundation cards in thirteen card sequence, disregarding suit, arriving at a card one less in value to the base card (four, five, six, seven, eight, nine, ten, jack, queen, king, ace, two, three).

Play out the cards from your hand one by one, discarding unplayable cards to a single heap. The top of this remains available, as usual.

All eight cards of the side reserves can be used at any time. Gaps here are refilled with the top card from the heap or with the next card from the pack.

The wheat-ear reserve differs slightly. The cards available for play are those nearest to you at the bottom of the layout. Removing one frees the card above. The wheat-ear is not replaced and quickly vanishes.

When all *your* cards are gone, turn over the heap and play it through again once more. A successful game will find the table empty of all save eight neat piles of thirteen cards.

GATE PATIENCE

One pack is needed for this and all cards face upwards.

Deal out ten cards, putting five in an upright column to the left and five in an upright column to the right. These are the 'gateposts', or reserve.

Now deal another two rows one above the other, four cards in each, between the parallel columns to represent the 'bars' of the gate. This is the tableau.

The object of the game is to remove the four aces to a line above the two bars of the gate, as they emerge in play, building upwards upon them to the kings, in sequence and suit.

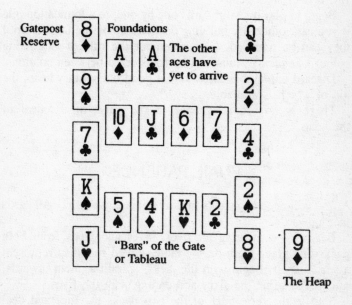

Fig. 21. Gate Patience.
The two of clubs is to be removed to its ace pile. If the eight of hearts is taken to fill the gap, the two of spades above is freed to be built upon the ace of spades.

Remove any foundation cards, together with anything to be built upon them, from the tableau or from the exposed cards at the base of the reserves to the side. (As always, this frees the card above for use.)

Build downwards in alternating colours on the tableau moving one card at a time and also using any suitable exposed cards from the base of the reserves.

Spaces made in the tableau are refilled with the next available card taken from the posts. When the gateposts have vanished − and this can happen very quickly at times, because the reserve is not replenished − use the top card from the, as yet, non-existent heap.

Begin to play out your cards one by one; to a foundation pile if you can, otherwise building downwards on the tableau until they can be removed. (Do remember the rule of alternating colour.) *Sequences* must not be transferred between columns.

Discard unplayable cards to that good old solitary heap, the top of which is available.

There is no second chance in the guise of a redeal of the heap.

SNAIL PATIENCE

You will need two packs for this imaginative game. All cards face upwards.

Begin by extricating all fives, sixes and jacks from both packs and place them on the table, coiled round to represent a snail's shell. Begin with the jacks, spiralling them inwards, afterwards using the sixes and ending with the fives.

Shuffle the remainder of the two packs together and deal four cards, horizontally, beneath the layout as a reserve. (See fig. 22.) The snail is now complete.

The object of the game is (a) to build downwards in suit on the fives to the king (five, four, three, two, ace and king) and (b) to build upwards in suit on the sixes, but ignoring the jack, to the queen (six, seven, eight, nine, ten and queen).

The reserve quartet can be used at any time. Deal the cards

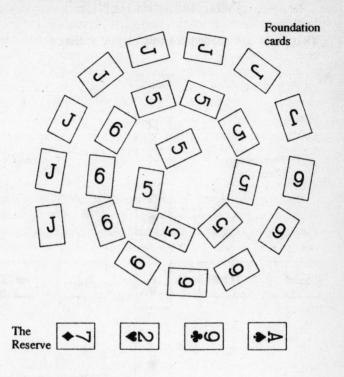

Foundation cards

The Reserve

Fig. 22. Snail Patience.
The layout – the seven of diamonds can be removed to a foundation card immediately, and replaced.

in your hand one by one, building on a foundation pile, hopefully.

Discard unplayable cards to a single heap, the top of which remains available.

Gaps made in the reserve are filled with either the next card taken from your hand or the top of that ever present heap.

One redeal is permitted. A successful game will show a snail shell made entirely of court cards. But if you find this game too easy, deal the cards only once.

(I have just been told that the Old English word for 'snail' is 'snaegel'. I didn't know that!)

WINDMILL PATIENCE

Two packs are needed for this classic Patience.

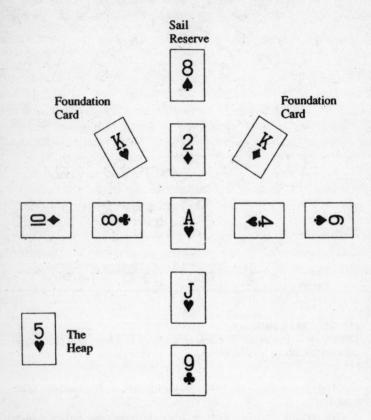

Fig. 23. Windmill Patience.
The layout. Only two of the four kings have emerged so far. The two of diamonds can be moved directly to the centre ace and the gap refilled from the heap.

Take an ace, of any suit, placing it in the middle of the table. This is the first foundation card.

Shuffle the two packs together and deal a reserve of eight

cards (face upwards, as are all the cards in this game): put two above, two below, two to the right and two to the left of the ace, representing the sails of the windmill.

As four kings, of any suit, emerge in play, place one diagonally between each of the sails as foundation cards. (See fig. 23.)

The object of the game is (a) to build four sequences of thirteen cards upon the ace in the centre, ignoring suit, to finish with a king (ace, two, three, four, five, six, seven, eight, nine, ten, jack, queen, king, ace, two, three and so on; the numbering is continuous). And (b) to build downwards on each of the four kings, ignoring suit, to the ace (king, queen, jack, ten, nine, eight, seven, six, five, four, three, two and ace).

Begin to play out the cards in your hand one by one, building wherever possible. Discard useless cards to a solitary heap, the top of which is there to be removed at any time.

All eight cards in the reserve are available. Spaces made here are to be filled from the top of the heap or, if that is exhausted or not yet begun, with the next card from the pack.

It is permissible to transfer the top card of a king foundation pile to the ace foundation pile, if you consider it advantageous,

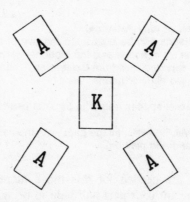

Fig. 24. Windmill Patience.
The happy ending.

but *never* remove the base card. I am afraid the opposite is not allowed: cards placed upon the centre ace are not removed.

No redeal of the heap is allowed. If you have been successful, the final layout will look like fig. 24.

QUEEN OF ITALY PATIENCE

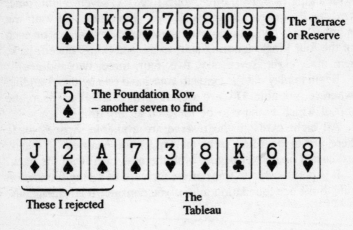

The Terrace or Reserve

The Foundation Row
– another seven to find

These I rejected

The Tableau

Fig. 25. Queen of Italy Patience.
(a) The six of hearts can be built upon the five of spades, seven of spades upon the six of hearts and the eight of hearts upon the seven of spades. The exposed card from the terrace – the nine of clubs – is placed upon the eight of hearts.

(b) Place the two of spades upon the three of hearts in the tableau.

As there is, as yet, no heap, fill the gaps with the next cards from the pack in your hand and play on.

Two packs are needed for this most interesting Patience. Good decisions on your part will help to bring this game to a successful conclusion. (Another name given to this is *Terrace*, a self-explanatory title, as you will see.) All cards face upwards.

When you have shuffled the packs together very thoroughly, deal a row of eleven cards at the top of the table as a reserve, overlapping them from left to right. (This is the Terrace.)

Below these deal a second row of four cards. Choose *one* of these as the first foundation card. The object of the game is to remove the other seven cards of the same value to the foundation row as they emerge in play. One must then attempt to build upwards, in sequence and in *alternating colours*, until each pile contains thirteen cards with the top card being one lower in value than the base card. The value of the cards is continuous, the ace being above the king and below the two.

Before deciding on your foundation card, look at the reserve to see what it contains. This row can be built *only* to a foundation pile, so think carefully. (In the example, I chose the five of spades as the first foundation. As you can see, the nine of clubs is the exposed card on the terrace; had I chosen either the two of spades, ace of spades or jack of diamonds as foundations, the cards in the terrace would have remained, unmoving, for a long time.)

If you deal two (three, or even all four) cards of the same value among these four cards, you will probably decide to keep both (or all) as foundation cards.

Take the rejected cards to begin a third row beneath the second and deal some more cards to bring the total number of cards in the bottom row to nine. This is the tableau.

Play what you can from the tableau to the foundations, building upwards in sequence and in alternating colours. In fig. 25, the foundation card is a black five. The sequence there will run thus: black five (five of spades), red six (six of hearts), black seven (seven of spades), red eight (eight of hearts) and so on until you reach a black four.

If you cannot play the cards in the tableau directly onto a foundation pile, play them on each other, building downwards in sequence and alternating colours until needed. Again, the value of cards is continuous so that if you have a red ace and a black king in the tableau, you can put the king on top of the ace. When building down on the tableau, it is better to place the cards in such a way that the value of all of them can be seen. Unfortunately, only single cards can be moved when building down, not sequences of cards.

The exposed card to the right of the reserve, or terrace, is built onto a foundation pile and nowhere else, as I have already said. Using this card frees the one beside it for use.

Spaces made in the tableau are to be filled from the heap if this is already in existence, from the top of the cards you hold if not.

Now deal out the pack one by one, building upwards on foundation piles where you can. Sheer impossibility? Then build downwards on a suitable card in the tableau.

Unplayable cards must be abandoned to a single heap, the top of which remains available throughout. There is no redeal.

If you were fortunate in your choice of foundation, the end of the game will find eight piles of thirteen cards beaming back at you, while the terrace has long since crumbled away!

STEP UP PATIENCE

You will need two packs for this game. All cards face upwards.

Shuffle the pack and deal out a row of thirteen cards, from left to right, in the centre of the table. This reserve is known as the 'landing'.

Take the next card from your hand and place it above the reserve. This card, of whatever value, is the first foundation card.

Your object is to find the other seven cards of the same value as they emerge in play, putting them in a line beside the first; and to build upwards upon each of the eight foundation cards, in sequence and suit, until each pile contains thirteen cards. For example: if the foundation is a queen, the sequence will run as follows — queen, king, ace, two, three, four, five, six, seven, eight, nine, ten and jack.

Deal another row, of nine cards, below the landing reserve and call this the 'staircase' or tableau.

This game has a chain of command. Cards can be removed to a foundation pile *only* from the landing reserve.

Found, or build on foundations, using whatever is possible from here and fill the spaces with any card you choose, taken from the staircase tableau. You don't have to fill a gap in the landing immediately it becomes vacant, nor do you have to fill a gap in the landing before you fill a gap in the staircase. But gaps in the *staircase* are *immediately* refilled with the next cards from the pack, or from the heap when this useful item comes into existence.

Cards in the staircase can also build downwards upon each other, in sequence and alternating colours, until they can step up onto the landing. Place the cards in such a way that their values can be seen. Cards must be moved singly, never in sequences. (Red king on black ace, black queen on red king and so on ...)

Begin to deal out the cards in your hand one by one. Build downwards on the staircase tableau, if possible, or discard unplayable cards to a single heap, the top of which remains ever available.

(*Please don't forget* to remove suitable cards from the landing reserve to a foundation pile when you can, filling the gap with any exposed card from the staircase!)

No redeal of the heap is allowed.

WANING MOON PATIENCE

Two packs are needed for this most appropriately named game. All cards are to be dealt face upwards.

Shuffle the packs together very thoroughly and deal out thirteen piles in the shape of a semicircle, three cards to each pile. This tableau represents the crescent moon.

Any aces found during this deal are taken out (replaced by the next card in the pack) and used to form a curved row beneath the tableau. (The remaining aces will take their places later as they emerge in play.) These are the foundation cards.

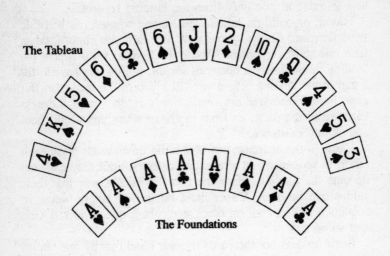

Fig. 26. Waning Moon Patience.
(a) The four of hearts can be placed on top of the five of hearts in the tableau.
(b) The three of spades is placed on top of the four of spades.

The object of the game is to build upwards, in sequence and in suit on the foundations, to the king.

The top card of each pile in the tableau is available for use and removing cards frees those beneath.

When all available cards in the original layout have been removed to the foundations, build *downwards* on the tableau, in suit, until they can be played off. (For example, seven of hearts upon the eight of hearts, four of diamonds on the five of diamonds and so on.) But please remember to keep the tableau piles meticulously tidy. You don't wish to see the cards beneath the top card and cheat inadvertently, do you?

Now deal out the cards in your hand one by one; either to the foundation piles or to the tableau. Discard unplayable cards to a single heap, the top of which always remains available.

Move cards singly, not in groups, between piles. A gap in the tableau is filled by any exposed card. You must decide whether it is wiser to choose the top card of the heap or the top card of a tableau pile for this.

As it is not permitted to play through the heap again, all cards having been dealt, a great deal of thought is needed to bring this game out. Should you have built correctly on each foundation pile to the king, the crescent tableau will have disappeared ... the moon has waned.

ROYAL RENDEZVOUS PATIENCE

Two packs are needed for this rather unusual Patience. Take the four twos from one pack, one from each suit, together with all eight aces from both. Place them as demonstrated: the eight aces in two rows of four, one beneath the other, at the top of the table. Put two twos to the right and two twos to the left of the lower row of aces. These are the foundation cards.

Shuffle the remainder of the two packs together very thoroughly, then deal out two rows of eight cards each beneath the foundation cards, as a reserve. (These do not overlap and all must face upwards.)

The object of the game is: (a) to build upwards in sequence and suit to the queens on the aces in the top row (ace, two, three, four, five, six, seven, eight, nine, ten, jack and queen); (b) to build, in suit, by steps of two upon the bottom row of aces to the king (ace, three, five, seven, nine, jack and king); and (c) to build, in suit, again by steps of two upon the twos (two, four, six, eight, ten and queen).

Each of the sixteen card reserve is available for immediate use. Build whatever you can from here to the foundations, filling spaces with the next cards from the pack.

Begin to deal out the cards in your hand one by one, to a foundation pile, with luck. Discard unplayable cards to a single heap, the top of which remains available for you.

Now the heap is in existence, fill gaps in the reserve with

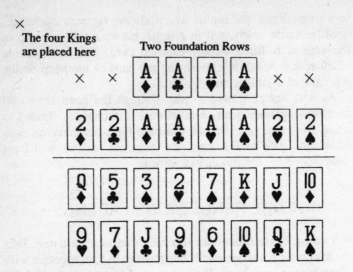

The four Kings
are placed here   Two Foundation Rows

The Reserve

Fig. 27. Royal Rendezvous Patience.
(a) The three of spades can be built upon the ace of spades in the lower foundation row immediately.
(b) The two of hearts is placed upon the ace of hearts in the top row. The two spaces will be filled by the next two cards from the pack, there being no heap, as yet.

the top card from here. Only when this has dwindled to nothing can one revert to using the next card from your hand, as before.

Four kings, one of each suit, remain unaccounted for. Place these above the appropriate two foundation pile when its twin has crowned his ace pile in the lower row.

There is to be no redealing of the heap at the end of the game.

If you are successful, all cards will have been gathered to the correct pile and the rows will read, from left to right, as follows:

Top Row: King, king, queen, queen, queen, queen, king, king.

Bottom Row: Queen, queen, king, king, king, king, queen, queen.

This scenario is not likely to be duplicated in real life nowadays!

DOUBLE OR QUITS PATIENCE

You will need one pack of cards for this Patience. It bears a vague resemblance to several games (distant cousin?), but its oddities single it out.

After shuffling the pack, deal out seven cards as a tableau as follows. (All the cards must face upwards.) Put three cards in a column to the left and three cards in a column to the right. They do not overlap. Between them, at the top, place the seventh card.

If you have dealt any kings, remove them to the bottom of the pack and replace them with the next card.

Now deal another card, the foundation card, putting it between the columns at the bottom. (Again, this must not be a king. If it is, replace it as before.)

The aim of the game is to build on the single foundation, doubling the value of each card, until all the pack has been gathered to it.

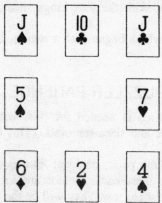

Fig. 28. Double or Quits Patience.
The two of hearts is the foundation card. The four of spades can be built upon it immediately and replaced by the next card from the pack. (There is, as yet, no heap.)

When the value of a doubled card exceeds twelve, subtract thirteen and play on. (The jack is worth eleven and the queen, twelve. Fortunately, suit is ignored.)

The sequence runs continuously: two, four, eight, three, six, queen, jack, nine, five, ten, seven, ace, two, four, eight and so on.

In the example shown in fig. 28, the foundation card is a two, but you will join the numbering wherever you came in. For example, if you dealt a queen, you would top this with a jack, followed by a nine, etc.

Play out the cards in your hand one by one, to the foundation pile if possible, or to a single heap, the top of which is always available.

Use the seven cards in the tableau whenever suitable, filling gaps made in it with the top card from the heap or your hand.

Kings play no part in this game. They can be used to fill a space in the tableau (*after* the original layout has been dealt) but move nowhere else.

The heap can be turned over and dealt out again twice when you have exhausted all the cards in your hand.

A successful game will have forty-eight cards built correctly on the foundation, with the four kings sitting disconsolately upon the table.

(The example, which began with a two, ended as it should, with an ace.)

PUZZLER PATIENCE

One pack of cards is needed for this, with all the twos, threes, fours, fives and sixes removed. (This is known as the piquet pack.)

After shuffling the pack, deal out four cards side by side, facing upwards. If these cards include any kings, put them in a line above the original row. They will be the foundations and will be joined by the remaining kings as they emerge in play. Fill any gap left by a king with the next card in your hand.

The object of the game is to build downwards in suit and sequence on the kings, to the sevens (king, queen, jack, ten,

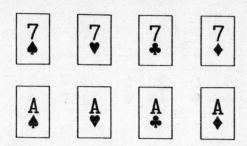

Fig. 29. Puzzler Patience.
A happy ending.

nine, eight and seven).

Begin to play out the cards in your hand, face up, onto the lower row. Stop between each deal of four cards to see if anything can be built on the foundation row. The removal of a card exposes the card beneath for use.

When the cards in your hand have been exhausted, gather up the lower piles from left to right and redeal them *once*.

If the game has been successful, each foundation pile will be topped by a seven, while the aces remain in a row below.

ONE FOUNDATION PATIENCE

One pack of cards is needed for this game. This Patience differs from most in having only one foundation, and beware … it is not as simple as it first appears!

Shuffle the pack and deal a row of seven cards side by side, face upwards. Deal a second row in the same way, overlapping the first; continue this until five rows have been dealt. This has the appearance of seven columns, the bases of each being the exposed cards.

Deal the next card, face up, onto the table. This is the foundation card. The object of the game is to gather all cards to it.

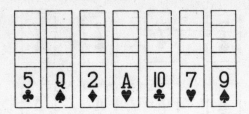

Fig. 30. One Foundation Patience.
The beginning. (All cards are facing upwards.)

The peculiarity of this game is that one may build, in sequence and regardless of suit, upwards *or* downwards, changing direction at any time. Exposed cards at the foot of the seven columns are used to build. Each time a card is used, the card above it becomes available for use. (If you use up all the cards from one column you don't replace them, but leave an empty space.)

For example: the foundation card in fig. 30 is a six. Either a five or a seven can be built upon it. One must plan ahead to avoid becoming blocked too soon. And here is the difficulty. An ace must *not* be placed upon a king, a king cannot be played upon an ace. (A queen is the only card permitted to be dealt upon a king and the two upon an ace.)

When further play from the columns is impossible, deal the next card from those held in your hand onto the pile. This is a new foundation.

Play available cards onto this until you become stuck, yet again. Deal another new foundation from those cards you hold and continue until all have been used.

The game is won if all fifty-two cards sit one upon another on the foundation.

DEAUVILLE PATIENCE

Why this game is named after the French coastal town I do not know; but I am positive that two packs of cards are required to play this excellent Patience. A great deal of thought is needed to bring it to a successful conclusion.

After the two packs have been well shuffled together, deal three overlapping rows with ten cards in each. All these cards face downwards. Deal a fourth row of ten cards to overlap the third, *this* row to face upwards. These are the 'exposed' cards.

Remove any aces that are immediately available in the exposed cards, placing them in a row below the tableau. The others will emerge in the course of play to join them. These are the foundation cards.

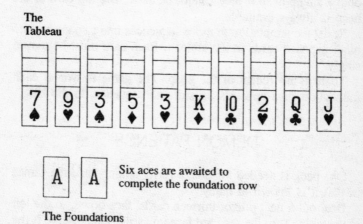

Fig. 31. **Deauville Patience.**

The object of the game is to build upwards, in suit and sequence, on each ace to the king.

When an exposed card has been removed, turn the card beneath over, so that it becomes available for use.

You can build downwards on exposed cards in the tableau in sequence but in alternating colours (red five on black six, black four on red five, and so on). When you do so, place the cards in such a way that the tops of any other cards there can be seen. This helps to plan the best move possible.

Play the cards in your hand one at a time. These, and all the exposed cards in the tableau, can be played in the following way:

(a) Immediately onto the foundation cards, hopefully ...

(b) If this is not possible, build downwards in sequence in alternating colours on the tableau until these can be moved to the foundations.

(c) Any exposed card can be used to fill a gap caused by the removal of all the cards in one column. This is very useful when a card is blocking play.

Cards played from those held in your hand can be discarded onto a single heap if they cannot be used. The top card of the heap is always available.

Resist the temptation to move sequences into a space or onto other exposed cards in the tableau. Each card must be moved singly.

There is no redeal of the heap. The game is won if each foundation runs upwards, in suit and sequence, to the king.

DEMON PATIENCE

One pack is needed for this; a rarity among Patience games in that it is known to many.

Deal out a neat pile of thirteen cards, face down, to the left of the table. Turn the top card face upwards. This reserve is the 'Demon' of the title.

Take the next card from those you hold, putting it face upwards at the top of the table as the first foundation card.

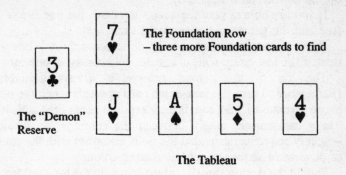

Fig. 32. Demon Patience.
The layout.

Beneath this deal a row of four cards as the tableau. Again, these must face upwards.

The object of the game is to take the other three cards, of equal value to the first, to the foundation row as they emerge in play: building upwards upon each, in sequence and suit, until each pile contains thirteen cards, thus absorbing every card in the pack. The top card will be one lower in value to the base. (As the example given is the seven of hearts, a successful sequence will run as follows: seven, eight, nine, ten, jack, queen, king, ace, two, three, four, five and six of hearts.)

You can build in a downward direction on the tableau, in sequence but alternating colours (e.g. red ace on black two, black king on red ace, and so on). Spread each column towards you; it helps!

A space in the tableau is filled with the top card of the reserve. The face-down card below it is then turned upwards for use.

Deal the cards from your hand in groups of three to a single heap, face upwards. When you have dealt the trio, look at the top card. Remove it, if possible, to a foundation pile (either founding it or building on it). Otherwise, build it downwards on the tableau until required.

If you *are* able to play the heap's top card, the one *below* is free and the game continues in the same way.

Pause to consider what is to be done between each deal of three. (The last group will, of course, only consist of one card.)

The top of the demon reserve is always available. (Remember to turn the face-down card upwards when the one above is removed.) So, too, is each exposed card of the tableau. These can transfer singly between the columns, or in any length of sequence, provided the 'join' complies with the rules of downward sequence and alternating colour.

Should the demon vanish, fill the gap with the top card from the heap *only*.

When the pack is dealt, turn the heap over and play it through again, redealing in batches of three as before.

This is done until the game is successful, or it becomes vividly apparent that the game is hopelessly blocked.

If the latter, there is nothing to be done but to gather up the entire pack and accept defeat gracefully. (Sweeping the cards before one onto the floor with muttered execrations is frowned on by most players!)

I wonder why this infuriating and aptly named game is so popular.

NAPOLEON AT ST. HELENA PATIENCE

The apparent simplicity of this Patience masks the difficulty of bringing it out successfully. (Like life, I suppose.)

It possesses several titles, *Forty Thieves* and *Big Forty* among them, but *Napoleon at St. Helena* seems to be the most popular.

Two packs are required and all cards must face upwards; one needs the addition of no *further* difficulty, goodness knows!

Begin by shuffling the two packs together and deal out four rows of ten cards as the tableau. Overlap them so that they resemble ten columns, with the value of each card clearly visible. If you deal any aces in these rows, remove them to use as foundation cards and replace them with the next cards in the pack.

The aim of the game is to take the eight aces, when they emerge, building upwards upon them in sequence and in suit to the king (ace, two, three, four, five, six, seven, eight, nine, ten, jack, queen and king). When found, put these foundation cards in a row above the tableau.

The card at the base of each column, having nothing upon it, is exposed and available for play and removing a card frees the one above.

Move any suitable card to the foundation row. Otherwise build downwards on other columns of the tableau in sequence *and in suit* (this is the stumbling block) until needed (eight of hearts upon the nine of hearts, seven of hearts upon the eight of hearts and so on). Move single cards only, not sequences.

When you have done all you can, deal out the cards you hold one by one, to the foundation piles or to the tableau. Discard unplayable cards to a solitary heap, the top of which is always available.

A space in the tableau, caused by the removal of a column, is filled with *any* available card.

No second chance in the way of a redeal is allowed.

EAGLE WING PATIENCE

One pack of cards is needed for this game. Begin by dealing out a pile of thirteen cards, facing downwards. For some reason, this is given the odd name of 'trunk', and is to be placed in the centre of the table.

Now deal out a further eight cards, facing upwards, as a reserve: four in a row to the left and four in a row to the right of the trunk. These are the eagle's wings.

The next card you deal will be the first foundation card and is placed above the reserve. (The other three foundation cards of the same value are to be moved into position beside it as they emerge in play.)

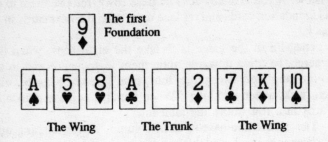

Fig. 33. Eagle Wing Patience.

Your aim is to build upwards, in suit, a sequence of thirteen cards ending with the card one lower in value than the card which began it. The example in fig. 33 shows the first foundation to be the nine of diamonds. This will run as follows — nine, ten, jack, queen, king, ace, two, three, four, five, six, seven, eight.

Deal out the cards in your hand one by one, building upon a foundation pile wherever possible. Discard useless cards to a single heap, the top card of which remains available to you.

Use the eight cards that form the wings for building on the foundation piles. Fill a vacancy here by removing the top card from the trunk and place it, face upwards, in the gap.

When you have dealt all the cards, the heap can be turned over and played through again, twice. I hope you find this leniency of some help. Usually, I do not!

FOLLOWING PATIENCE

One pack of cards is required for this game, together with a good memory and the ability to remain unflustered.

All cards face upwards; additional difficulties are not needed.

Begin by dealing a tableau of six cards, placed in a row from left to right.

The object of the game is to remove the four aces to the top of the table as they surface in play, building upwards in sequence upon them to the king.

That is simplicity itself. Here is the hard part: only a club is to be placed on a heart, a diamond on a club, a spade on a diamond and a heart upon a spade. (Thus, ace of spades, two of hearts, three of clubs, four of diamonds, five of spades, six of hearts, seven of clubs, eight of diamonds, nine of spades, ten of hearts, jack of clubs, queen of diamonds and king of spades.)

Remove from the tableau all aces, and cards to be built upon them, to the foundation row. Fill spaces with the next card taken from those you hold.

Build downwards on the tableau if possible, following the same required arrangement of suits as above, i.e. club on heart, diamond on club, spade on diamond and heart on spade.

Any length of sequence can be moved between columns, provided the rotation of diamonds, spades, hearts and clubs is emblazoned on the memory.

The obvious difficulty will be that, in removing cards to the foundation piles, only one card can move at a time, the order being back to front.

Play out the cards in your hand one by one, building wherever possible and discarding useless cards to a single heap, the top of which is there to be used at any time.

Do not forget to fill spaces in the tableau with any available exposed card taken from the heap, hand or base of a tableau column.

When the pack is exhausted, turn over the heap and play it through once again in the same way as before.

A successful game will show the four foundation piles crowned with a king of the same suit as the ace at the base!

This *is* a difficult Patience and I have brought it out only rarely; I wish you greater success.

LIMITED PATIENCE

Two packs are needed for this difficult game. Shuffle the cards together very thoroughly and deal out three rows of twelve, all cards to face upwards. These tableau cards must not overlap.

Take away any aces in the bottom row and put them in a line at the top of the table. (Hopefully, any other aces *will* emerge − or be freed from the top two rows − during play!) The object of the game is to build upwards, in sequence and in suit, upon these foundation cards to the king.

The base card of each of the twelve 'columns' of the tableau is exposed and free for use. Removing a card frees the one above it. Do any building possible onto the foundations, then begin to play out the cards in your hand.

Those unable to be placed can be discarded to a single heap or built downwards on any exposed card in the layout, but it is here that the difficulty begins. One is very 'limited' in the way this is to be done. Only a single card, of the same suit and one lower in value, can be put upon another, taken either from those you hold, the top of the heap or another exposed card in the tableau (four of diamonds upon the five of diamonds, ten of clubs upon the jack of clubs and so on).

And here is the tricky part ... This pair are now *totally* immovable until they can be played to their foundation pile. They must not be built upon further or, even worse, removed to a space. A space made by the emptying of a column is filled by any available card, if that is what you wish. But beware, it is sometimes wiser to leave the gap empty.

When all the cards have been dealt, there is a second chance for success. Turn the heap over and take the top four cards from it. Place the four cards in a line facing upwards and, if possible, play them to a foundation pile or pair with another on the tableau or put them into a space. (Now you see how useful spaces can be.) This will set the game moving once more, if luck is with you.

Anything taken from this reserve of four cards is to be replaced by the next card (or cards) from the heap. When *no* card of this quartet can be moved, the game has ended. No further helps are permitted.

MARIA PATIENCE

This two-pack game is simple to describe, but difficult to bring out successfully.

After shuffling the two packs together, deal out four rows of nine cards, all to face upwards.

One is supposed to keep the rows separate, but I always overlap them so that the tableau resembles nine vertical columns of four, with the value of all these cards clearly visible.

The aim of the game is to take the eight aces as they emerge in play (putting them in a row at the top of the table), building upwards upon them, in sequence and in suit, to the king.

Remove any aces among the exposed cards (those with no other cards upon them, initially at the base of the columns) and anything that can be built on them. In this way the cards above are freed for use. Then build downwards in sequence upon the columns of the tableau, in alternating colours, until needed (black six on red seven, red five on black six, etc.). Any *single* exposed card in the tableau can be moved to another column, provided that the rules of sequence and colour are observed.

When nothing more can be done, play out the cards in your hand one by one. Place them on the foundation piles wherever possible, or build them downwards on the tableau.

A gap in the layout, caused by the removal of a column, is filled by any exposed card.

Discard unplayable cards to a solitary heap, the top of which is always there for you to use.

As no redeal of the heap is permitted, a great deal of forward planning is needed to free vital cards and bring this classic Patience to a satisfactory end.

Q.C. PATIENCE

Two packs are needed for this difficult Patience, named after a Victorian member of the Bar (perhaps Sir Edward Marshall Hall?) who played this when Whist was not possible. Whether the barrister devised the game is unknown.

After the obligatory thorough shuffling together of the packs, deal out twenty-four cards in four rows of six; this is the tableau. (All cards in this Patience face upwards.) Overlap the rows so that the layout resembles six vertical columns.

The object of the game is to remove the eight aces to the top of the table as they emerge in play, building upwards on these foundation cards in sequence and suit to the king.

Remove any aces that happen to be skulking among the exposed cards in the bottom row, with anything that can be built on them. This frees cards above them for use.

Single available cards (not sequences) can be transferred to other suitable columns, building downwards on the tableau in sequence and suit until they can be played to a foundation pile.

Begin to deal out the cards from your hand one by one. If a foundation pile is not yet attainable, try to play them into the tableau. Discard useless cards to a single heap, which has a greater importance than in other games.

If a column is emptied, the gap must be filled with the top card from the heap. A second annoying rule requires the top card of the heap to be built onto a foundation pile in preference to a duplicate card at the base of a tableau column.

This is remarkably effective in blocking the game and raising the blood pressure.

It is allowable to turn the heap over, the pack in your hand having been dealt, to play it through again once. (However, truth compels me to add that this is not permitted by some.)

TRIPLE LINE PATIENCE

Two packs are needed for this plain, no-nonsense game. Begin by shuffling the packs together, afterwards dealing out, face upwards, three rows of twelve cards each, from left to right, as the tableau. Overlap the rows so that the layout resembles twelve upright columns of three.

The object of the game is to take the eight aces as they surface in play (putting them in a row at the top of the table), building upwards on these foundation cards, in sequence and in suit, to the king.

Remove all aces in the exposed cards (those in the bottom row of the tableau with no other card upon them) and anything that can be built on them. Yes, this releases the card above for use!

Any *single* exposed card in the tableau can be built downwards in suit onto another column until needed (seven of hearts onto the eight of hearts, six of hearts onto the seven and so on ...). The removal of *sequences* of cards would make this game easier, but is not allowed.

When nothing more can be done, play out the cards in your hand one by one, hopefully to a foundation pile, otherwise building downwards in suit on the tableau.

Discard useless cards to a single heap, the top of which remains available.

Should all the cards in a column have disappeared, fill the gap with a single card, taken either from the top of the heap or the next card from those in your hand.

The heap can be turned over and played through once more when all your cards are dealt. Despite this grudging second chance, the game is surprisingly difficult to bring out.

SIX BY SIX PATIENCE

One pack of cards is needed for this unusual and difficult Patience.

Deal out, facing upwards, a tableau of thirty-six cards in six rows of six, overlapping them so that they resemble six perpendicular columns.

Remove any aces from the exposed cards at the base of each column (automatically freeing the card above), placing them

above the layout. All other aces are put in the foundation row
as they emerge or are released from the tableau during play.

Your aim is to build upwards on the aces to the king, in
sequence and in suit.

Deal out the cards in your hand one by one, building them
upwards onto the foundation piles where possible or building
downwards onto the tableau, in sequence but ignoring suit,
until they are needed.

Any exposed card in the tableau can be moved singly
between columns, provided the rule of downward sequence is
kept. But a *sequence* of cards (more than one) can only be
moved if all the cards in it are of the same suit and placed on
an exposed card of correct number *and suit*. These are rare!

This game is odd in that unplayable cards do not form a
heap; they are placed one by one on to the first tableau column
to the left, regardless of value, spreading downwards. The card
at the end of this column − or any sequence if the rules are
followed, as above − is always available for you to use.

A space caused by the removal of a tableau column is to be
filled by any available card or a downward sequence in suit.
(You guessed!)

With no redeal allowed, great care is necessary to prevent
the game becoming hopelessly blocked.

If fortune is with you, the end of the game will see all the
cards gathered to the four foundation piles, topped by their
king.

3

QUIET PLEASE, BRAIN AT WORK

The games in this section need slightly more concentration to bring out.

It is less easy to blame an ill-shuffled pack for failure, although there are *always* pitfalls to be discovered skulking among the unseen cards.

SIR TOMMY PATIENCE

This is supposed to be the first Patience ever invented, but who Sir Tommy was I do not know. (Many people who think that Patience has only *one* game know this one.)

The object of the game is the usual one − to build on the aces up to the king − but it is not necessary to follow suit, i.e. diamonds on diamonds, clubs on clubs, as with some games of Patience. The number on the card is the only thing of importance.

You will need one pack of cards. Shuffle these well and begin to lay out four piles facing upwards. You can place the cards on whichever pile you like as the piles do not have to contain an equal number of cards − see below. Remove the four aces as they appear. The aces are placed in a line below the four piles and if there are any twos, place these on the aces, followed by threes and fours and so on, as far as possible.

If the cards cannot be placed on an ace pile, put them on the ordinary piles above as you please. But take care. It is a good idea to put the court cards on one pile so that the low cards, so necessary to be immediately available if the game is to be successful, are not blocked.

You must not transfer a card from one ordinary pile to another. It must stay in the pile chosen until it can be placed on an ace foundation pile in the usual way.

If you have not been able to place all the cards on an ace foundation by the time all the cards have been dealt, the game has been a failure. (Shuffle again and better luck next time!)

COLOURS PATIENCE

One pack of cards is needed for this simple, but aggravating, game.

Begin by dealing out the pack, face upwards, into up to six heaps. Pile these as you please; the top cards are always available for use.

You are looking for a two, three, four and five to become the foundation cards. The two and four must be one colour (suit is not important) and the three and five the other. Obviously, the first foundation card to emerge dictates the colour of the others.

When found, put these cards in numerical order, and side by side, at the top of the table.

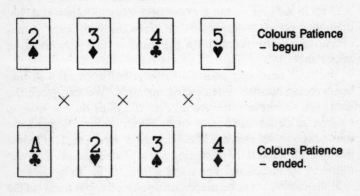

Colours Patience
– begun

Colours Patience
– ended.

Fig. 34.

The object of the game is to build upwards on these, in colour and in thirteen-card sequence, to a card of a value one below the foundation card.

Build from the cards you hold and watch the tops of the heaps with an eagle eye. (Discard cards with some care, or you will find yourself becoming hopelessly blocked.) One must *not* move a card from heap to heap, only to a foundation pile.

Redealing the heaps is not allowed. A successful game shows the four foundation piles topped by an ace, two, three and four, respectively.

ALTERNATE PATIENCE

One pack of cards — and a great deal of space — is needed for this game. (All cards face upwards.)

Remove the ace of diamonds, the king of clubs, the ace of hearts and the king of spades and put them in a row at the top of the table. Each of these is to head a vertical column of thirteen cards, none of which should overlap.

The aim of the game is to build upwards in sequence and alternating colour on each ace to the king (black two on red ace, red three on black two and so on) and downwards in sequence and alternating colour on each king to the ace (red queen on black king, black jack on red queen, etc.).

Deal out the cards in your hand one by one, building whenever the opportunity arises. Discard unplayable cards to one of four heaps which can be piled as you please. As always, top cards remain available for you to use. But you can only move them to a foundation pile, not from one heap to another.

When all the pack has been dealt, the heaps can be gathered up and played through once again. (Resist the urge to shuffle them!)

The end of a successful game will show four vertical columns, thirteen cards in each, filling the table. The ace columns will end with a red king; the columns headed by a king end with a black ace.

HIGGLEDY-PIGGLEDY PATIENCE

Two packs of cards, well shuffled together, are needed for this messy and enjoyable game.

Scatter the packs higgledy-piggledy all over the table, ensuring that all the cards are facing downwards. Clear a space in the middle (you will now wish that you had chosen to play this game on the floor) and choose any card to be a foundation card. If you have drawn a queen, for example, you will build on her, ignoring suit and colour, as follows: king, ace, two, three, four, five, six, seven, eight, nine, ten and jack on top.

(The other seven cards of the same rank are built on in the same way as they are found.)

Begin to turn the cards over at random. If they can be placed on a foundation card, all well and good. If they cannot, form four heaps, piled as you please, with the top cards only available for use. These top cards can only be placed on the foundation piles, not moved from one heap to another.

When all the scattered cards have been turned face upwards and no card can be placed from the heaps, take the heap on the left and play it out, hopefully onto one of the eight foundations, or onto the three remaining heaps in rotation. Next take the third heap (again the one on the left) and play it out onto either the foundation cards or the two heaps that are left, then play out one of these heaps onto the foundation cards or onto the one remaining heap.

If the sequences on the foundation cards have not been completed after the last heap has been played, you have been unsuccessful in your attempt.

PUSS IN THE CORNER PATIENCE

One pack of cards is needed for this game. Remove the four aces and put them on the table, face up, in the shape of a square. Follow this by shuffling the pack.

The object of the game is to build upwards in sequence (ace, two, three, four and so on) and in colour (red card on red card, hearts or diamonds, and black on black, spades or clubs regardless) to the king.

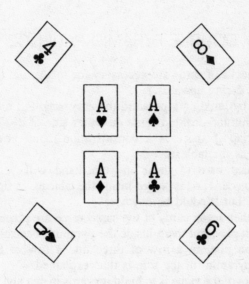

Fig. 35.   Puss in the Corner Patience.

Play out the cards in your hand one by one, face upwards. Those unable to be placed on a foundation pile are put into one of four heaps, piled as one chooses. (It is very helpful — but not always possible — to avoid putting a higher card upon one of lower value.) The top cards of these are always available for moving to a foundation pile; they may not, however, be moved from one heap to another.

The heaps are positioned at an angle, one to each corner of the square, mirroring the game for children which lends its name to the Patience.

All cards having been dealt, pick up the heaps in a clockwise direction and, *without* shuffling them, play your 'new' pack out once again. No more chances are given. I hope the ending was happy.

DOUBLE PYRAMID PATIENCE

Two packs of cards are necessary for this game. (All cards are dealt facing upwards.)

Begin by building a pyramid the easy way. Put one card at the summit and deal ten cards on either side of it. (The cards can overlap if space is a consideration.) You now have a pyramid as the tableau.

The next card of those in your hand will be the first foundation card and is placed inside the tableau. In fig. 36, this is a five, but it could be *anything!*

The other seven cards of the same value are placed as they emerge in play. Put them inside the pyramid, beneath the first foundation pile, in a row of three and a row of four. The 'double pyramid' of the title is thus explained.

The aim of the game is to build upwards in suit and sequence upon the foundations, ending with a card one less in value to the card at the bottom of the pile (for example, five, six, seven, eight, nine, ten, jack, queen, king, ace, two, three and four).

Use any suitable card in the tableau for building, at any time. A card removed from here is never replaced.

Play out the cards in your hands one by one. If they are of no immediate use, pile them as you choose onto one of four heaps that form the base of the pyramid. The top cards of these remain ever available for moving to a foundation pile; they may not, however, be moved from one heap to another.

No redeal is allowed. A successful game will find each of the eight foundation piles containing thirteen cards and the large, outer pyramid gone.

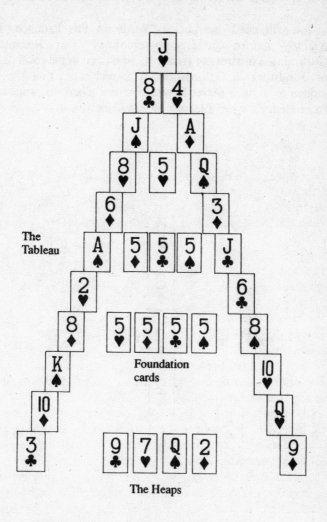

Fig. 36.   Double Pyramid Patience.
A demonstration of the layout. (The six of diamonds and the six of clubs
can be played onto the foundations from the tableau.)

ROSAMUND'S BOWER PATIENCE

You will need one pack of cards for this Patience. This quaintly named game commemorates 'Fair Rosamund' Clifford, the mistress of Henry II, who lived in the royal palace of Woodstock in Oxfordshire. A legend states that she was hidden away in a secret bower within a maze, to protect her from Henry's wife, Eleanor of Aquitaine.

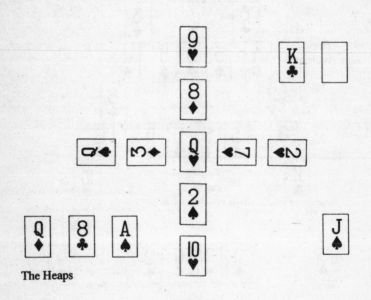

Fig. 37. Rosamund's Bower Patience.
The beginning.

Remove from the pack the queen of hearts (or Rosamund), the king of clubs and the jack of spades. The queen is placed in the centre of the table with eight cards as guards around her: two above, two below and two on either side. All these cards face upwards.

The king of clubs is placed above these to the right. Beside him is dealt a pile of seven cards, facing downwards, as additional guards.

The jack of spades is placed at the bottom of the table. Using the cards in one's hand, build on the jack of spades in a downward direction, paying no attention to suit (jack, ten, nine, eight, seven, six, five, four, three, two, ace, king, queen and so on).

Three heaps are formed of cards not used immediately, piling them as one pleases. The top card of each heap is always available for use but must not be moved to the top of another heap.

If there is a suitable card on the *outside* of the eight cards protecting the queen, this must be used in preference to the cards in your hand or on top of the heaps. Fill the gap immediately with the card on top of those lying face down beside the king of clubs.

It is allowable to gather up and replay the heaps three times. (These must *not* be shuffled.)

The game has succeeded if the king of clubs and the queen of hearts sit triumphantly atop the jack pile.

GEMINI PATIENCE

Two packs of cards are needed for this game. As with all games in this book, *shuffle the cards well* before beginning. Take the first four cards of different values and place them face up on the table. Leave a space between them as twin cards, of any suit, must be placed beside each as they turn up.

Deal out the cards in your hand onto one of five heaps, piling them as you please. When you deal a card of the same value (of any suit) as one of those first four cards (its twin), place it in the space left for it. Then, when a card one degree higher (of any suit) than this twin pair emerges, place it above the pair. Once you have *that* card's twin placed beside it, you then build upwards, again not paying any attention to suit (any four on any three, any five on any four, etc.). In each case, before further

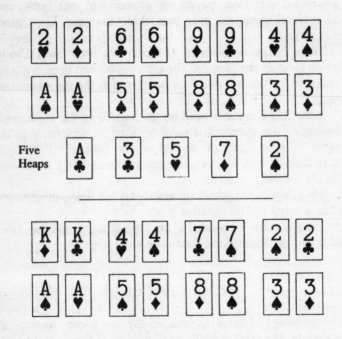

Fig. 38. Gemini Patience.

building upwards is allowed, cards placed above the original twins must also have their twins beside them (e.g. in the example shown in fig. 38 you would need a three on top of both the two of hearts and the two of diamonds before you could put a four on either of them).

Only the top card of each heap is available for use (which must not be transferred between heaps) so great care must be taken in laying out cards on the heaps, otherwise one becomes hopelessly stuck.

A successful end to the Patience shows the original twins, each with a pile above it crowned with the card next *below* it in value. If one is not successful immediately, a second chance is given by gathering up the heaps, unshuffled, and playing these cards off again; only two heaps may be formed this time and no further attempt is allowed.

This game can be made even more perplexing by playing one of the twin cards upwards and the other downwards. The end result is the same, but very difficult to achieve. Do not try it if there is anybody 'helping' you!

THE LADY OF THE MANOR PATIENCE

You will need two packs of cards for this game. Remove the eight aces, putting them to one side momentarily. Shuffle the remaining cards, then count out four piles of twelve cards each, laying them in a row face upwards. See fig. 39 overleaf.

Now place the eight aces in a row beneath these piles. The remaining cards are arranged in a semicircle above the four piles, according to their value, from the two to the king. Now begin to build on the aces (two, three, four, five and so on) without regarding suits. Take the cards from the semicircle to do this until an appropriate one appears on one of the four piles. This must be taken in preference to those in the semicircle, the object of the game being to use all the cards in the four piles. If you do not succeed in this, the game has failed.

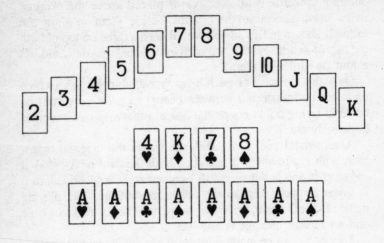

Fig. 39. The Lady of the Manor Patience.

MISSING-LINK PATIENCE

One pack of cards is needed for this. It is important to shuffle the cards very thoroughly before attempting it.

Cut the pack and remove one card from the middle *without looking at it.* Put it to one side, face down; this is the 'missing-link' of the title.

The object of the game is to remove the four aces, as they emerge in play, and to build upwards upon each in sequence and suit to the king.

Deal the cards in your hand one by one, all facing upwards, to an ace pile (if you are lucky) or discarding unplayable cards to one of up to seven heaps. These heaps are to be formed as you think best. (Obviously it is not wise to put a high card upon one of lower value and same suit, if this can be avoided.) The top of each heap remains available for use throughout the game but cannot be transferred to another heap.

A vacancy caused by the removal of an entire heap is filled

by any exposed card or the next card from the pack.

When you can play nothing more, turn the 'missing-link'. Hopefully this will revive the game. There is no redeal.

A successful game will show four piles of thirteen cards, each topped with a king.

SNAKE PATIENCE

You will need two packs of cards for this game, which are to be well shuffled together.

Take out a complete sequence of cards, from the ace up to the king, without taking any regard as to the suit, and lay them out in the form of the letter 'S', beginning with the seven as the end of the tail and six as the snake's head.

Now deal out the rest of the cards, building upwards on the base cards (any eight on the seven of diamonds and so on, any jack on the ten of clubs, any two on the ace of diamonds etc.).

Obviously the first cards are easily placed, but as the game progresses some cards cannot find their correct position on the piles. Two heaps of whatever size can be made with these until they can be used; take care not to block cards that you will soon need. Also, a card placed on a foundation pile cannot be moved onto another, so do not be tempted to build too quickly.

If the game works out successfully, the snake will be composed of an ace as the tip of the tail, running in sequence up to the king as its head. (See the second 'S' of fig. 40.) Each pile will contain eight cards.

If you yearn to give yourself a headache, the game can be made more difficult.

Lay out the foundation cards in diamonds. The second layer must consist of spades, the third layer of hearts, the fourth of clubs and so on. As there are eight cards in the final piles, the top layer will be a sequence of clubs.

With this version, four heaps are allowed. Once you have dealt out all the cards, the heaps can be picked up, well and truly shuffled and dealt out again. This may be done twice in

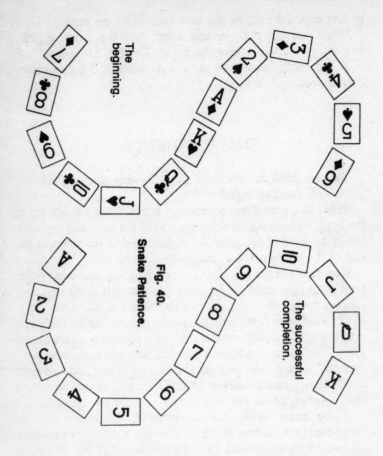

The beginning.

Fig. 40.
Snake Patience.

The successful completion.

the course of the game. However, it is still very difficult to avoid having cards hopelessly blocked. (Also, I find it extremely difficult to remember whether I am supposed to be laying down a red or black card when I am in full swing, but that is just me, probably!)

EIGHT ACES PATIENCE

You will need two packs of cards for this Patience. Remove

the eight aces and place them in two rows of four. These are the foundation cards and are to be built up in suit until each pile is topped by the king.

Play the cards (which should have been well shuffled, naturally) from your hand onto one of the foundation cards or onto one of six heaps, only the top card of which is available for use. One must *not* move a card from heap to heap, only to a foundation pile.

A vacancy caused by the removal of an entire heap is either filled by any exposed card or by the next card in the pack. But it is not necessary to fill gaps immediately if this moves the game along.

When all the cards have been dealt out and the game has ground to a halt, remove the top card from each of the heaps and place it face down beneath its pile. This may restart the game. Play on until you are stuck again, then repeat the placing of the top card face down under its pile. When you arrive at the cards which have been turned over, they can be played normally, if possible.

If you only have one card in a heap and the game has ground to a halt, you may turn the card over and place another exposed card on top of it. But, if you wish the game to be more difficult, you should leave the card face upwards. You can choose either of these methods, but must not swap between the two.

The top cards can be removed only twice. No further chances are allowed.

LABYRINTH PATIENCE

One pack of cards is needed for this Patience. Remove the four aces from the pack and place them in a row at the top of the table, face upwards. These are the foundation cards.

The object of the game is to build in sequence and in suit on these cards, up to the king.

Begin by shuffling the pack thoroughly. Now deal eight cards in a row from left to right, facing upwards, beneath the foundation row.

Play any suitable card onto the appropriate ace, then fill any gap (or gaps) thus produced with the next card taken from those you hold in your hand.

When nothing more can be played, deal another row of eight cards immediately below the first and play as before; with one important exception. Do not fill in any gaps you may make. This is done in the first row only. In such a way does the labyrinth effect appear.

Continue playing in the same way until all the cards are used.

Exposed cards, those at the top and at the bottom of each column, are available for play onto the foundations after every deal.

(Using a card from the top row releases the card immediately below it. In the same way, a card taken from the bottom row frees the card above it for use.)

Should the Patience grind to a halt, it is permitted to take one card from *anywhere* to build on a foundation. Hopefully, this should set the game moving again.

There is no redeal. The game is won if all the foundation cards have been built in sequence and suit up to the king.

WHEEL OF FORTUNE PATIENCE

Two packs of cards are required for this game, but they must not be shuffled together.

Begin by dealing out a circle of sixteen cards from the first pack. (All cards in this Patience face upwards.)

If there are any kings or aces, remove them to the centre of the circle, putting them in two parallel lines as foundation cards. Immediately fill any gaps made with the next cards from the pack. The other kings and aces are to be placed correctly as and when they emerge.

The object of the game is to build upwards on the four aces, in sequence and in suit, to the kings and to build downwards on the four kings, in sequence and in suit, to the aces.

Move whatever else you can from the tableau to the

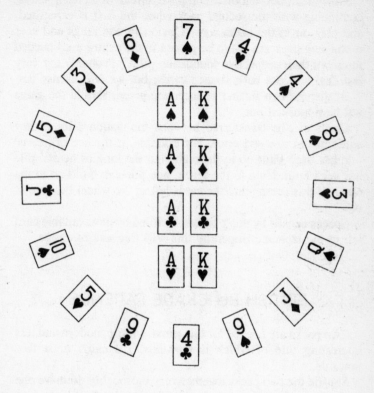

Fig. 41. Wheel of Fortune Patience.
A demonstration of the tableau, all the foundation cards having emerged.

foundation cards, always refilling spaces from the cards in your hand.

When there is no more to be done, deal a second complete circle of sixteen cards upon the first. Use these cards to build upwards or downwards as before, remembering to remove aces or kings to the centre. The taking of a card frees the one beneath for use. Again, a space made in the layout must be filled by the next card from those you hold.

Now deal out another complete circle of sixteen cards, continuing with the second pack when the first is exhausted, and play on in the same way. (Obviously, the kings and aces in the new pack are not to be placed in the centre until needed to crown their respective foundation piles.) Probably the very last deal will not have sixteen cards, but we will excuse it.

At the end two further chances are given, should the game not have worked out.

Cards can be transferred between foundation piles *if* they agree in suit and sequence. For example, if the ace of hearts' pile has been built up to the eight and the king of hearts' pile has been built down to the seven, one pile can build on to the other, if this means that the cards left in the wheel become of use.

Spaces caused by this play can be filled by *any* available card left in the tableau. Hopefully this will free any blockage.

BRITISH BLOCKADE PATIENCE

Two packs are needed for this game, a more modern and less interesting title of which is *Parallels*. All cards must face upwards.

Shuffle the two packs together very thoroughly. Remove one ace and one king from each suit, putting the four kings in a vertical column to your left and the four aces, in the same fashion, to your right. Allow plenty of space between the two. These are the foundation cards.

The object of the game is to build upwards, in sequence and suit, upon the aces to the appropriate king and downwards, in sequence and suit, upon the kings to the appropriate ace.

Deal ten cards in a row between the parallel kings and aces as a reserve. Pause to consider whether any of these can be used for building. Fill any spaces made with the next cards to be dealt from the pack.

When nothing further can be done, deal a second row of ten cards below the first, but do not overlap them.

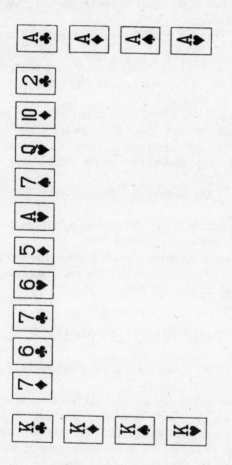

Fig. 42. British Blockade Patience.
The two of clubs and the queen of hearts can be removed to their foundation piles. Gaps are to be filled immediately from the pack.

The cards in both rows are now available for play to the foundation piles. Continue to fill the gaps with the next cards taken from those you hold.

Deal a third row of ten cards below the second, play having come to a standstill.

Now only the top and bottom row are available. The second row finds itself blockaded, the title of the Patience is vindicated, and a card here is only freed for use when the card immediately above or below it is taken away. Build everything possible, refilling gaps as before.

Blocked again? Deal a fourth row of ten below the previous three. Now there are *two* inner rows awaiting the order of release. Play on, remembering that cards in the inner rows must have a free edge above or below (or both) before you can use them.

No redeal of the reserve is allowed when the pack is exhausted.

Running a blockade has its difficulties, so too has this game − although it's not as frightening!

A truly horrible variation does not allow the top row to possess *any* available cards until all the pack has been dealt. The less said about *that* the better.

GRANDFATHER'S PATIENCE

Two packs are necessary for this most venerable of games. All cards are to face upwards.

Shuffle the packs together and deal out two rows of ten cards each, horizontally, parallel to each other, as a reserve. Remove any kings or aces as foundation cards (but only one from each suit, the duplicates are treated in the same cavalier fashion as any other value). Put the kings in a line above the reserve and the aces in a line below the reserve. Also take anything that can be built on them. Fill gaps, as throughout this game, with the next cards from the pack.

The object of the game is to take the kings and aces as they emerge in play; building upwards in sequence and suit upon the aces to the king and building downwards on the kings, in sequence and suit, to the ace.

Deal the cards you hold one by one, building on a foundation pile if possible. Unplayable cards can be placed in one of two ways: either discarded to a single heap, the top of which is always available or, if you choose, played to the reserve, *not more* than one card upon each of the twenty. If you do this, only the uppermost card can be used.

This *can* be most helpful in bringing the game to a successful conclusion, but great care must be taken in avoiding the inadvertent blocking of vitally needed cards.

The heap can be turned over and played through once more, when all the cards have been dealt.

If, near the end of the game, you have used up all the heap and you have spaces in the reserve, you may fill these spaces with top cards of the reserve.

A successful game will find four piles in the row above, each topped by an ace, while the four piles below are crowned with a king. And the reserve has vanished away ...

IMAGINARY THIRTEEN PATIENCE

I like this Patience very much, although it appears rather complicated at first. It is very satisfying when it ends well.

You will need two packs of cards for this game. Place on the table eight cards of any suit, running in sequence from the ace to the eight. Below these put a card of any suit which is double the value of the card above. (The jack is valued at eleven, the queen at twelve and the king at thirteen.) So put a two below the ace, an eight below the four, a queen below the six, and so on. A brief difficulty, speedily resolved, is caused by the doubling of the seven and the eight. This is where the *Imaginary Thirteen* of the title is used. Two sevens are fourteen, for which no card exists. If you deduct the imaginary thirteen from fourteen, you are left with one. Therefore place an ace beneath the seven. The same thing happens with the eight. Two eights are sixteen; the imaginary thirteen is

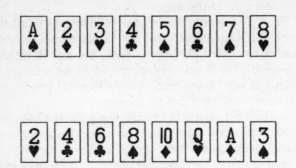

Fig. 43. Imaginary Thirteen Patience.
The game now ready to begin.

deducted and so a three of any suit is placed below the eight.

Begin to deal out the pack in your hand. If you deal a card with a value equal to the total of the upper and lower cards, place it on the card in the lower row. For example, place a three (one plus two) below the ace, a six (two plus four) below the two, a queen (four plus eight) below the four, and so on. Again, when the value of the upper and lower card exceeds thirteen, deduct the imaginary thirteen and use a card to the value of the amount left over. A queen and a five would total seventeen, so deduct thirteen and place a four on the lower card.

If a card cannot immediately be placed onto one of the lower cards, place it on one of four heaps, reserving one of these heaps solely for the kings.

Take the cards for the lower row from the heaps whenever possible before taking from the cards you hold; in that way, you have more chance of bringing the game to a successful conclusion.

Continue adding to the lower row until both upper and lower card total thirteen, and place the king on the lower card. If you can do this on each of the eight piles, the game has been worked out correctly.

JUBILEE PATIENCE

Two packs of cards are required for this game. It was in 1887 that Queen Victoria celebrated her Golden Jubilee. Today a similar occasion would be marked by the sale of lurid T-shirts, souvenir tea-towels and colour supplements galore. *Then* a loyal populace devised games of Patience in her honour, of a difficulty to make one tear one's hair!

If you are feeling strong enough to make the attempt, begin as follows.

Remove all eight kings and put them, facing upwards, in a row at the top of the table.

The aim of the game is to build upwards on the kings to the queen, in suit, in the following way: king, ace, jack, two, ten, three, nine, four, eight, five, seven, six, queen.

Begin to deal the cards in your hand; either onto the king piles if you can, or to one of four heaps. (I think it wiser to reserve one of the heaps for the queens alone and beware of blocking cards soon needed.) As always in these games, the top card of each heap is available for use. But, you are not allowed to move it from heap to heap — only to a king pile.

When you have played all your cards, turn over and gather up the heaps, without shuffling them, and redeal. This can be done twice.

That doyenne of Victorian writers on the game, Miss Mary Whitmore Jones, has the last word: ' … Success is difficult to attain; it is not the lot of every queen to have a Jubilee.'

STONEWALL PATIENCE

One pack is needed for this austere little game. Whether the Patience was named as a compliment to Thomas J. Jackson, one of the Confederate generals of the American Civil War, who stood with his brigade 'like a stone wall' at the Battle of Bull Run in 1861, I know not.

Shuffle the pack very thoroughly — an absolute necessity here — and deal out six rows of six cards each as the tableau.

The first row, together with the third and fifth, must face downwards, while the second, fourth and sixth rows face upwards. Overlap the rows so that they resemble six vertical columns.

The object of the game is to remove the four aces to a row at the top of the table as they emerge in play, building upwards upon these foundation cards, in sequence and in suit, to the king. Unfortunately, if you deal an ace into any row except the sixth row of the tableau, you have to wait until it can be released.

The remaining cards are dealt in two rows of eight, facing upwards, beneath the tableau. This is your reserve.

All sixteen cards here, together with exposed cards at the base of the columns, are available. (When a card which faces down is uncovered, turn it over and carry on.)

Move anything possible to a foundation pile; with the remaining cards, build *downwards* on the tableau in sequence and *alternating* colours until they can be played off.

A single card, or any length of sequence, can be transferred to the base of another column, provided the join is correct.

An empty column is filled with any available single card or sequence, but the reserve is not to be replaced.

I hope that you will not find this game *too* annoying! I always feel a great satisfaction when I bring it out, which is not often, I must admit.

MISS MILLIGAN PATIENCE

Two packs are required for this classic game. No collection is complete without the maddening Miss Milligan, although some might be happy to see her go!

Shuffle the two packs together very thoroughly and deal out a row of eight cards, facing upwards, from left to right. This is the beginning of the tableau.

The aim of the game is to move the eight aces, or foundation cards, into a line at the top of the table as they emerge in play, building upwards upon them, in sequence and in suit to the king.

Remove any aces, together with any cards that can be built upon them, from the first row of the tableau. Follow this by dealing a second row of eight cards upon the first, all the cards in this Patience facing upwards.

Overlap the cards which remain, or any spaces made, ensuring that the values of all cards can be easily seen. View the tableau as eight upright columns.

Pause to consider what is to be done. The exposed cards in the tableau can be built downwards in sequence and *alternating* colours upon exposed cards in another column until they can be removed to the foundation piles (red seven on black eight, black six on red seven and so on).

There is no limit to the number of cards in a sequence which can be removed from one column to another, provided that the rule of alternating colour and downward numbering is observed.

An empty column can be filled only by a king, or a sequence of which the king is the beginning.

Deal another row of eight cards as before and play on. (Obviously, the columns will be of unequal length.)

No move is to be made until each deal of eight cards is set down.

An unusual help, called 'waiving', is permitted when the last eight cards have been placed. Any one exposed card at the base of a column can be put to one side, thus permitting the removal of cards trapped above it. The card taken must eventually be played back into the game, either to the tableau or a foundation pile.

'Waiving' can be done as many times as you wish, but the card removed must find a new home; you cannot 'waive' a second card if the first is 'homeless'. If it cannot be replaced, the game is a failure, because the eight foundation piles will not have gathered all the cards to themselves beneath the king.

STRATEGY PATIENCE

One pack is necessary to attempt this marvellously infuriating game, devised by Mr. A. Morehead and Mr. G. Mott-Smith.

Shuffle the pack very thoroughly, then begin to deal the cards (face upwards) as you decide, to any one of eight heaps.

Remove the four aces to a row at the top of the table as they emerge in play.

The object of the game is to build upwards upon each ace, in sequence and in suit, to the king.

No card can be built upon a foundation ace until the *whole* pack has been dealt.

Now your strategy (or, in my case, lack of it) in distributing the cards between the eight heaps is made clear.

With luck, you should be able to lay the exposed cards from each heap, freeing the card beneath as you remove the top one, on the foundation cards up to the king, without becoming blocked.

To attain this happy state of affairs, it is wiser to keep one of the eight piles exclusively for the kings and queens and not to put a higher card upon a lower one unless forced to.

The only comfort I can give is that practice makes the game a little easier ...

INTERREGNUM PATIENCE

This game requires two packs of cards, and some thought to bring out! Even the title is something of a puzzle. The only historical Interregnum I know in English history is the gap between the execution of Charles I in 1649 and the accession of Charles II in 1660, so gloomily filled by Cromwell.

Begin by shuffling the two packs together very thoroughly and deal out eight cards, in a row from left to right, at the top of the table. They are called the indicator cards and face upwards, as do all the cards in this game.

Leave sufficient space beneath these for the foundation cards to be placed as they emerge during play. Then deal out a bottom row of eight cards.

Your aim is to find the card one step higher in value than each indicator card.

Building upwards on each one, ignoring suit, in thirteen card sequence until its respective indicator card can be used to crown the pile. (These elusive eight foundation cards take up their position as the second, or middle, row directly below their appropriate indicator cards.)

For example, should the first card in the top row be a two, the foundation card beneath will be a three. The sequence will run as follows: three, four, five, six, seven, eight, nine, ten, jack, queen, king, ace and, finally, the indicator card two.

All eight cards in the bottom row are available for use, either as a foundation card or for building.

When you can do no more, deal out another eight cards upon the bottom row, covering remaining cards or spaces, and play as before. (To remove a card frees the one beneath for use.)

Continue, pausing between each deal of eight cards to build upon the foundation piles whenever possible, until all the cards in your hand have been exhausted.

No redeal is permitted. A successful game will find you able to play out all the cards in the bottom row onto the foundations, and permit yourself a pat on the back.

SQUARING THE CIRCLE PATIENCE

You will need two packs of cards for this game, together with a clear head. (At least all the cards face upwards ...)

Remove the four aces from one pack — one of each suit — and put them in a square upon the table. These are the foundation cards.

Now shuffle the two packs together very thoroughly and deal out a reserve of twelve cards, encircling the aces.

Your object is to build simultaneously upwards *and* downwards upon each ace, in suit, until the pile is topped by its twin, the second ace. The sequence runs as follows: ace, king, two, queen, three, jack, four, ten, five, nine, six, eight, seven, seven, eight, six, nine, five, ten, four, jack, three, queen, two, king and ace.

Begin by removing anything suitable in the twelve card reserve to a foundation, filling spaces with the next card from

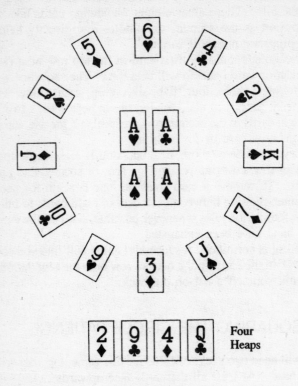

Fig. 44. Squaring the Circle Patience.
The layout. The king of spades is to be built upon the ace of spades, the space being filled by any top card from a heap.

those you hold.

When there is nothing more to be done (although the reserve cards are always eager to be used, throughout the game), play out your cards one by one. Hopefully, *some* will find a home on the foundation piles immediately. Discard unplayable cards to one of four heaps, piling these as you choose in the most judicious manner. The top card of each is available for use, but cannot be moved from heap to heap.

Fill any gap you make in the reserve from now on with the

top card from a heap. If you are in the happy position of having made the heaps disappear in play, fill spaces again from the cards you hold.

Having exhausted the packs, gather up the four heaps from left to right and turn them over, dealing them out again as before. This is your last chance to square the circle ... a mathematical conundrum which the ancient Greeks proved impossible, but not in our case.

MARTHA PATIENCE

One pack is needed for this satisfying game. After shuffling the pack very thoroughly − absolutely vital − remove the four aces and put them in a line, face upwards, at the top of the table.

These aces are the foundation cards and the object of the game is to build upwards, in sequence and in suit, until a king crowns each pile.

Deal out four rows of twelve cards: the first and third rows are to face downwards, the second and bottom rows to face up. Overlap these cards (the tableau) so that they look like twelve vertical columns.

The card at the base of each column, having nothing upon it, is 'exposed' and available for use. Removing a card frees the one above. (If *that* faces downwards, turn it over with a nonchalant air and play on!)

Move all possible exposed cards to the foundation aces, then build downwards in sequence and alternating colours onto the tableau columns until they can be played off (black five on red six, red four on black five and so on).

Any one exposed card, or a sequence of whatever length, can be played to another column *if* the rule of alternating colours is remembered.

A gap in the tableau, caused by the removal of a vertical line, is not to be filled in quite so lax a fashion. Only *one* available card is placed there − not a sequence − as a new beginning.

With careful consideration, this game should end well.

MOUNT OLYMPUS PATIENCE

In the prosaic world, Mount Olympus is a trifle under 10,000 feet in height and situated in the north-east of Greece. To most of us, as to the unknown Victorian composer of this game, it is the home of the ancient Greek gods and goddesses. The layout of the game shows this very well.

Two packs of cards are needed and the cards face upwards.

Begin by removing all the aces and all the twos from both packs. Put them in a semicircle, alternately, at the top of the table. These sixteen foundation cards represent the cloud which shrouds Mount Olympus.

The object of the game is to build upwards, in suit, on these in the following way:

ace, three, five, seven, nine, jack and king;

two, four, six, eight, ten and queen.

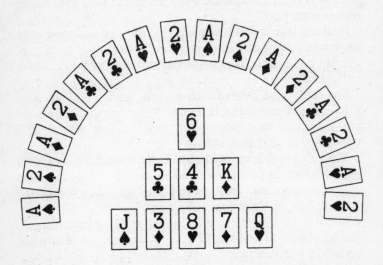

Fig. 45. Mount Olympus Patience.
The beginning – the three of diamonds can be placed on the ace of diamonds immediately, and the four of clubs on the two of clubs. The gaps will be filled by the next cards from those in your hand.

Shuffle the remainder of the two packs together and deal out a triangular tableau of nine cards beneath the arc of the foundation row: one card in the top row, three in the second row and five in the third row. (This symbolises Mount Olympus.) *Do* allow plenty of space between the nine cards.

Remove suitable cards in the layout to the foundations; otherwise, build downwards on the tableau cards, in suit and by twos (seven of diamonds on the nine of diamonds and so on). Make a downward column of each so that you can see the values.

Exposed cards can be moved singly between tableau piles, or in any length of sequence provided the 'join' is correct, until they can be played to the foundation piles.

Gaps must be filled immediately by the next card from those *in your hand*. Don't be tempted to do anything else, whatever the provocation from blocked cards!

When the game has stuck, deal another nine cards, one to each tableau pile, and play on.

There is no second chance, in the shape of a redeal, when all the cards have been played. But, if when you have dealt out all the cards you are left with gaps in the tableau, you can move the top card from another pile to fill the spaces.

A successful ending will show the foundation piles topped by kings and queens — gods and goddesses peering benignly from their home.

FLY PATIENCE

Two packs of cards are needed for this game. Shuffle the two packs together, first removing the eight aces. These are placed in a row upon the table and become the foundation cards.

Now deal a pile of thirteen cards face down and put them to your left. Having done this, turn the top card of this pile face up. For some inexplicable reason, this is the 'fly' of the title.

The aim of the game is to build upwards on the foundation cards (in sequence, but paying no regard to suit) to the king.

As one would expect, the top card or 'fly' is always available

for use. Once removed, the card beneath is turned face up.
Should the entire pile be played off, it is not replaced.

Begin to play the cards in your hand one by one. Any of no
immediate use are discarded on up to five heaps, piled as one
pleases. Use the top cards of these heaps as soon as it is
feasible. But, do not move a card from heap to heap.

(Try to avoid placing cards of a higher value on those of
lower rank as the heaps form; one can become stuck very
easily.)

No redeal is permitted. Unless the 'fly' and all the other
cards have been correctly absorbed onto the foundation piles,
the game is not a success, unfortunately.

LA BELLE LUCIE PATIENCE

One pack is needed for this unusual and visually pleasing
Victorian Patience. As it also requires thought and planning to
bring it to a happy ending, one cannot ask for more!

(Do allow yourself plenty of room in which to play this
charming survivor from more spacious days.)

Play out the cards, face upwards, in groups of three, each
trio overlapping one another in the form of a fan. (There will
be eighteen of these groups in the tableau, but the last 'fan' will
have one card only.)

The object of the game is to take the four aces as they emerge
in play, building upwards on them in sequence and suit to the
king.

In this game, the 'exposed' card is that card uncovered at the
end of a fan. Should any aces be seated there, desperate to
catch your eye, put them in a line at the bottom of the table.
These are the foundations. (The removal of a card releases the
one beneath for play.)

Build any suitable exposed card onto a foundation pile. If
this cannot be done, build downwards in sequence *and* suit,
which adds greatly to the difficulty, upon the end of another
fan until needed. (A fan removed during play is not replaced.)

Should the game become stuck, pick up all the cards not yet

correctly placed on a foundation pile and shuffle them thoroughly. Redeal this 'new' pack into fans of three, as before. (Obviously, the last fan of this redeal may consist of only one or two cards.)

You may replay the cards twice, but no *further* chances are given.

An easier version of this game, named *Trefoil*, begins with the four aces placed as foundation cards at the start of the game. The tableau comprises sixteen fans, with three cards in each.

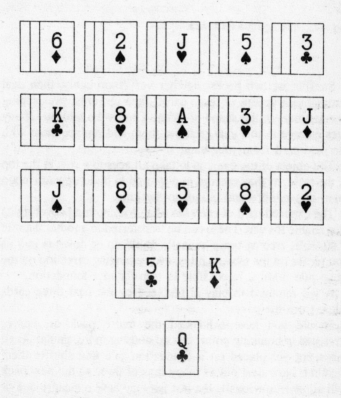

Fig. 46. La Belle Lucie Patience.
The ace of spades is immediately available, together with the two of spades to be built upon it. (All cards face upwards.)

INTELLIGENCE PATIENCE

Two packs and a large table are needed for this colourful Patience.

Fig. 47.   Intelligence Patience.

Shuffle the two packs together very thoroughly, then deal out eighteen groups of three cards (face upwards, overlapping one another) in the shape of a fan. This is the tableau. If any aces emerge in this deal, remove them and replace them with the next card from your hand.

The object of the game is to take all aces to a row at the top of the table, as they emerge in play, and to build upwards upon them in sequence and in suit to the king.

The exposed card of each fan (that with nothing covering it) is available for use. These can be transferred to another fan pile if suitable, freeing those beneath. Build up or down *in suit* as you please on the tableau piles, even changing direction on the same pile, until it is possible to transfer to a foundation.

A fan removed in play is replaced by the next three cards taken from the pack.

Should you have exhausted the entire pack or, nerves stretched to breaking point, can do nothing more, gather up all cards not yet placed on a foundation pile and shuffle them together. Now deal out as many fans of three as the new pack will allow — obviously, the last fan may have a meagre one or two cards in it — and play on. (Do not forget to extricate any aces from the redeal.) This can be done twice in all.

4

PER ARDUA

These games enable one to see all the cards at a glance, played out upon the table.

Careful planning and full deliberation can bring a seemingly impossible game to a successful ending, which is very satisfying.

RAGLAN PATIENCE

One pack of cards is necessary for this game. The Patience differs slightly in that all cards are dealt out, face up, before the game begins. (I find it easier to play this game with miniature cards ... or perhaps my tables are smaller than average!)

Begin by removing the four aces, putting them to your right on the table. These are the foundation cards.

The object of the game is to build upwards in sequence and in suit on these aces to the king.

The pack having been shuffled, deal six cards as a reserve, lining them up below or to the side of the foundation cards, as you please.

The remainder of the pack is placed in the following way. Deal seven overlapping rows of cards with nine cards in the top row, eight in the second, seven in the third and so on, decreasing by one in each row until the seventh, which contains three cards only.

The tableau has the appearance of nine columns, the card at the base of each column being the 'exposed' card. These exposed cards and any of the six cards in the reserve are

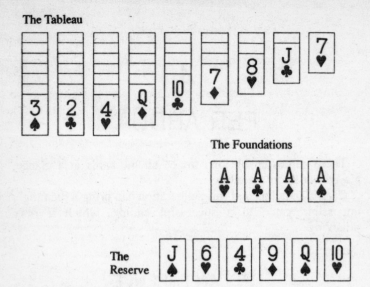

Fig. 48. Raglan Patience.
The beginning. (All cards face upwards.)
(a) The two of clubs can be removed to its foundation card;
(b) The three of spades can be placed upon the four of hearts;
(c) The reserve jack of spades is to be placed upon the queen of diamonds;
(d) And the ten of hearts upon the jack of clubs.
A very good start.

available for building onto the aces, if possible. (The cards in the reserve are not replaced when removed.)

When you have moved all possible cards to the foundation piles, build in descending sequence and alternate colours on the exposed cards of the tableau (red six on black seven, black five on red six and so on) until they can be played to the foundation piles. Cards must be moved singly, not in groups, however tempting. Cards from the reserve can also be used for building.

Should a column be removed, *any* exposed card can be put there, but it is not obligatory to fill the gap.

A successful ending has all cards sitting quietly in sequence and suit on the foundations, a king on top of each pile.

FLOWER GARDEN PATIENCE

One pack is needed for this Patience. All cards are dealt face upwards.

Begin by playing out thirty-six cards, making six rows of six cards, the rows to overlap. This is the tableau or 'garden' of the title.

The sixteen cards that remain, called the 'bouquet', are placed above the six columns of the garden in the shape of a crescent.

The object of the game is to remove the four aces as they emerge in play, building upwards in sequence and in suit upon them until they are crowned by the appropriate king.

When released, these foundation cards are put in a row below the garden.

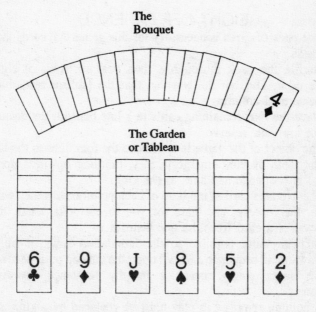

Fig. 49. Flower Garden Patience.
The beginning. The aces as yet unfound. (All cards face upwards.)

The base of each column in the tableau is the 'exposed' card and, yes, is available for play. The removal of a card frees the card beneath for use.

Any card in the bouquet is instantly available for building and is not replaced.

Moving cards one by one (including cards in the bouquet), build either upwards upon a foundation pile or, if impossible, build downwards in sequence upon the columns of the tableau, ignoring the suit, until they can be played off (any eight on any nine, any seven on any eight and so on).

If all cards in a column have been removed, the space can be filled with any available card. (Obviously, it is sensible to move a king into a space whenever possible. The cards blocked by him are then set free.)

The game is won if the garden and bouquet have gone and the four foundation piles are topped by their kings.

EIGHT OFF PATIENCE

One pack of cards is necessary for this game. All cards face upwards.

Shuffle the pack thoroughly, then deal six rows of eight cards each. Overlap the rows so that the tableau resembles eight vertical columns.

Place the four remaining cards in a line beneath the layout. These are your reserve.

The object of the game is to remove the four aces to the top of the table as they emerge in play, building upwards upon each, in sequence and suit, to the king.

The exposed card at the base of each column, together with all in the reserve, are there for you to use. (As usual, the removal of a card frees the one beneath.)

Take anything possible to the foundation row; or build downwards in sequence *and suit* upon the tableau until needed. Move cards singly, never a lengthy sequence however tempting.

A column removed in play must be replaced by a king, no other value will do. (And this does not mean that you can extricate the royal personage from the obscurity of cards awaiting release; the space remains until he becomes available.)

This is followed by a helpful rule. *Any* exposed card can be transferred to the reserve row as you choose, provided the quantity of cards here does not exceed eight (as in the title). Good luck!

SALIC LAW PATIENCE

Two packs of cards are needed for this game. The Salic Law, not repealed in Spain until 1830, gave preference to a male succession to the throne. (Very stupid when one considers that the most stable and charismatic sovereigns in recent history have been women!) This explains why the eight queens are removed before the game begins and placed in a row, side by side and facing upwards, at the top of the table. Their splendid

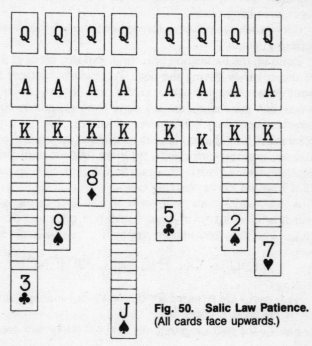

Fig. 50. Salic Law Patience.
(All cards face upwards.)

isolation ensures that they take no part in the game at all.

Shuffle the packs together thoroughly and put one king at the extreme left, leaving a generous amount of space between it and the row of queens. (*All* cards face upwards.)

Play out the cards you hold, one by one upon the king, overlapping downwards so that the value of each card can be seen. Remove all aces as you deal, placing them in a row below the queens. The aces are the foundation cards.

The object of the game is to build upwards on the foundations, in sequence but paying no regard to suit, to the jacks. As you deal out each card check whether it can immediately be placed onto a foundation pile. If it can, check whether any other exposed cards (those at the ends of a column) can be moved onto a foundation pile.

When you come to a *second* king, put it beside the first and deal out downwards on the second king until the third pops up. Continue dealing downwards on the last king found once all eight have been placed.

(Obviously, the columns spread beneath each king will be of differing length.)

Build on the foundation piles from exposed cards at the end of the columns during the deal. Afterwards continue in the same way. (*Only* exposed cards can be played onto the foundation piles and must not move from column to column, however necessary.) Whenever possible, play to empty a column. A king that is alone is considered an 'empty' column and any exposed card can be put there (but not until you have dealt out all the cards). This enables the game to keep moving, as it removes cards blocking play.

A successful game will show a row of queens, beneath which will be a row of eight foundation piles topped by the jacks. The third and bottom row will consist of eight kings.

HOUSE ON THE HILL PATIENCE

Two packs are required for this space-consuming game. All cards are to face upwards.

Shuffle the packs together and deal out thirty-four groups of three cards, overlapping each trio in the shape of a fan. The thirty-fifth and final fan has only two cards in it, but is none the worse for that.

(If, having a literal mind, you have built the tableau in the shape of a pyramidal hill as the title suggests, the small fan is placed at the apex.)

The object of the game is to remove the eight aces as they surface in play, and to build upwards upon each of these foundation cards, in sequence and suit, to their kings.

The top card of each fan is there for your use, its removal frees the one below.

Transfer anything possible to the foundation row; otherwise build downwards on the top cards of the tableau, in suit, until those cards can be played off. Move one card at a time, *never* a sequence.

A fan which disappears is not replaced. There is no redeal. A successful game will show eight piles of thirteen cards, topped by a king.

STALACTITES PATIENCE

One pack is needed for this appropriately named Patience. All cards must face upwards.

Begin by shuffling the pack, afterwards dealing four cards to the top of the table as foundation cards. Turn them on their sides, so that you will have a constant visual reminder as to their value and where to stop! The other cards played onto these are piled in the usual way (i.e. upright).

The object of the game is to build upwards upon these horizontal cards, ignoring suits, until each pile contains thirteen cards. You may build in steps of one or two, but whatever you choose to do must apply to each of these foundations.

In the example given in fig. 51, I decided to build in twos, so the sequence on the first card will run as follows: ten, queen, ace, three, five, seven, nine, jack, king, two, four, six and eight.

Deal out six rows of eight cards each, overlapping the rows so that the layout resembles eight upright columns.

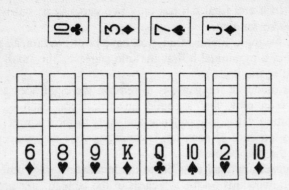

Fig. 51. Stalactites Patience.
(All cards face upwards.)
(a) The queen of clubs can be removed to the first foundation pile;
(b) The nine of hearts will be built upon the seven of spades;
(c) The jack of diamonds will gather the king of diamonds, followed by the two of hearts, to it. An excellent start.

Exposed cards at the base of each column are available for play and their removal frees the card above. A column emptied is not to be refilled.

While there is no building downwards on the tableau, help is at hand. Two cards can be taken from *anywhere* in the columns and kept until they can be built onto a foundation pile. This is invaluable in unblocking trapped cards, and can be repeated three times in all.

I hope this is of use. *Stalactites Patience* is not as easy as it appears at first glance.

SCOTCH PATIENCE

Perhaps this Patience should be more properly named *Scottish Patience*, but it is so venerable that it would take somebody braver than me to tamper with it.

Only one pack of cards and a good memory are necessary for this.

Deal out a tableau of eighteen piles, face upwards, in three rows of six. Sixteen piles contain three cards each, the seventeenth and eighteenth have two in them.

As you deal, *do* try to remember where the aces are placed, because the object of the game is to free them in play and build upwards upon them in sequence, but in alternating colours, to the kings (red ace, black two, red three and so on). As the aces surface, put them in a row below the tableau.

Begin by removing any aces that are among the exposed cards, together with all cards that can be built on them, thus freeing those beneath.

Build downwards on the tableau, ignoring suit and colour (any queen on any king, any jack on any queen, etc.), moving cards singly from pile to pile until they are needed on the foundations.

Used piles are not replaced and there is no redeal. I confess that I have been unable to progress further than three completed sequences. Try as I may, the fourth continues to elude me.

BAKER'S DOZEN PATIENCE

One pack of cards is needed for this, and a lot of thought. (When the pillory, or worse, was the punishment for short weight in loaves of bread, the bakers protected themselves by selling thirteen for the cost of twelve. The thirteenth loaf was called the 'vantage'. I do not suggest that the Patience is either that ancient or invented by a baker!)

Shuffle the pack thoroughly and deal out four rows of thirteen cards, face upwards. Overlap them so that the tableau resembles thirteen vertical columns and the value of all cards can be seen.

The merciful originator of this Patience dictates that the kings must be transferred to the tops of their respective columns — which eases life a great deal. If you have more than one king in a column, put one king above the other. With them safely penned, the game can begin.

Your object is to place the four aces, as they emerge in play, in a row above the tableau. Build upwards upon these foundations, in sequence and in suit, until the piles are crowned with a king.

Take any aces available in the exposed cards (an exposed card being one at the base of a column with nothing upon it) and any cards that can be built on them, moving one card at a time. The removal of a card frees the one above it.

When nothing more can be played, build downwards on the tableau columns in sequence, but ignoring suit, until these cards can take their positions on the foundation piles (any five on any six, any four on any five). But you must only move one card at a time and not a sequence of cards. A gap in the tableau is not to be refilled.

If the game comes out well, you may wish to attempt a variant, called *Good Measure*. (Does this title refer also to bread, or something more exotic?)

Good Measure is played in the same way, differing a little in the original layout. Two aces are removed before the game begins, awaiting the other two, and placed above the tableau. This consists of five overlapping rows, ten cards in each.

BELEAGUERED CASTLE PATIENCE

One pack of cards is needed for this game. The layout is as depicted in fig. 52, with all the cards facing upwards.

The four aces are removed from the pack and placed in a column down the centre of the table.

To the left and to the right of each ace deal a line or 'wing' of six overlapping cards, so that only the card at the end is totally exposed, though the value of each card can be seen.

The object of the game is to build upwards in suit on the aces to the king (ace, two, three, four, five, six, seven, eight, nine, ten, jack, queen and king).

Only the exposed card on the end of each wing can be played, either immediately onto the correct ace or onto the end of another wing.

If built onto a wing, the sequence is built downwards with

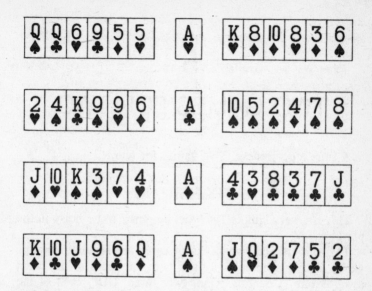

Fig. 52. Beleaguered Castle Patience.
The layout.

no regard to suit – any five on a six, any jack on a queen – until cards necessary to the ace piles can be released. Only one card can be moved at a time.

A space having been created by the removal of all the cards in one wing, any exposed card can be put there. In this way a card which is blocking play can be transferred, freeing those beneath for use.

It is very important to plan ahead if one wishes to bring this Patience to a successful conclusion.

In fig. 52 the two of clubs can be put onto the ace of clubs immediately; the jack of clubs onto the queen of diamonds, the seven of clubs onto the eight of spades, enabling the three of clubs to join the two on the ace of clubs and so on ...

A shamefaced but truthful footnote: I have *never* been able to bring this Patience to a successful ending. On confessing this to a friend, he played and concluded it in ten minutes! I retain my belief that it is a difficult game.

5

TWO GAMES FOR TWO

A little togetherness. Two games for two.

HASTY PATIENCE

This is a very simple Patience, but tends to be noisy in the playing!

Two players and two packs of cards are required for this game. Each player holds a pack with the backs of the cards towards him. Counting 'One, two, three, GO!', each of the players begins to deal the cards into a heap in front of himself, the cards now facing upwards on the table, obviously. As the aces emerge they are placed in a line in the centre, and covered with cards in upward sequence, regardless of suit. The player who completes a pile with the king must remove it from the table. As the game must be played as fast as is possible, decorum goes out of the window and the cards are thrown on the floor.

If each player places a card on a pile simultaneously, the first card on the pile (i.e. the one underneath) stays there, while the card on top is taken back and placed at the bottom of the cards that player holds.

Unfortunately, if a player places a card onto a foundation pile and this leaves a suitable card on top of his heap, he cannot touch the card on top of the heap, but must continue dealing out the cards in his hand.

When a player has dealt out all his cards, he should pick up the heap and deal it out again. The player who gets rid of all his cards first is the winner. (And do not forget to retrieve all cards from the floor, behind the sofa or in the goldfish bowl!)

SYMPATHY PATIENCE

This Patience requires two players and two packs of cards. It also requires a lot of space as the piles must not be crowded together.

Each player takes a pack of cards. The first deals his cards in three rows of six piles. All except the last two piles contain three cards; those two have only two cards each. All cards are placed face down.

The second player also lays his cards out in the same fashion, but with the top card of each pile facing upwards.

The first player, whose cards are all hidden, turns over the top card on the first pile. If there is a duplicate facing upwards, in the cards of the second player, both cards are removed and the next card on the first pile of the first player is turned face upwards. If there is no duplicate to be found, that card is left facing upwards. The first player now goes onto the second pile and the move is repeated.

When all the piles of the first player have been worked through, the first player will have cards facing upwards on top of all his piles, while the second player will have as many piles with cards facing downwards as duplicates have been found.

The second player now turns up, one at a time, the top card in each pile that is facing downwards to see if it is a duplicate of one of the first player's cards. If it is, both cards are removed and the next card on that pile is turned face upwards; if it isn't, the second player carries on and turns over the top card of the next pile which is facing downwards.

The game continues, with the players taking it in turns to turn over their cards to check for duplicates, until there are no more hidden cards to turn over.

If all the duplicates are found, then both players are in sympathy; if not, the game has failed.

INDEX

(The number bracketed beside the game shows the number of packs required to play it.)